Second Grade Bound 2

Thinking Kids™
An imprint of Carson-Dellosa Publishing LLC
P.O. Box 35665
Greensboro, NC 27425 USA

Thinking Kids™
An imprint of Carson-Dellosa Publishing LLC
P.O. Box 35665
Greensboro, NC 27425 USA

Printed in the USA • All rights reserved.   ISBN 978-1-4838-1286-1
01-046151151

Table of Contents

Second Grade Bound: What Your Child Needs to Know

Second Grade Bound is designed for the child who is entering second grade. It starts out by reviewing skills your child may have learned in first grade and gradually advances on to skills he or she will likely learn in second grade. Reviewing and practicing these important skills will ensure greater understanding and an advantage for the grade ahead.

This workbook addresses important language arts, math, and reading skills your child needs to know to succeed in the classroom and beyond.

This guide provides background information about the skills and subject areas that are important for success in the coming school year. Tips are provided for helping your child develop in each curricular area.

Reading and Language Arts

Reading
Teach reading with texts that fit your child's ability and interests, using a variety of books, children's magazines, Web sites, charts and graphs, and other materials. Make regular visits to your local library so that there is always something interesting to read at your home. Choose two kinds of books—books at or near your child's reading level that can be read independently, and those at a higher reading level for read-aloud time.

Even after your child becomes an independent reader, it will benefit him or her greatly when you read aloud together every day. Read a variety of books aloud, including realistic stories, fantasy stories, adventure stories, mystery stories, and nonfiction books about topics of interest.

Before reading, activate your child's prior knowledge of the book's subject. For example, discuss the stages of a butterfly's life cycle and what caterpillars eat before reading Eric Carle's *The Very Hungry Caterpillar*. During reading, stop occasionally to make predictions, discuss the meaning of new words, and discuss confusing parts. After reading, talk about what you liked and didn't like about the story.

Look for opportunities to teach the following skills as you read with your child.

- Word Recognition and Vocabulary Development
  When your child encounters a new word in reading, encourage him or her
  to use different strategies to find its meaning:
  —Look at the surrounding text for context clues
  —Look at the syntax of the sentence and use the position of the new word as a clue
  —Sound out the word phonetically
  —Ask an adult or other knowledgeable person to provide a definition
  —Look up the word in a dictionary

- Phonics
  Look for opportunities to teach the following skills in the context of words found
  in books: beginning, middle, and ending sounds and spellings; consonant blends
  and digraphs (as in **tr**ain and **sh**ip); rhyming words; and long and short vowel
  sounds and spellings. Keep lists of words that have different vowel sounds: **short
  a**, **long a**, **short e**, **long e**, etc. Encourage your child to break longer words into
  syllables, identifying one or more vowel letters in each syllable.

- Reading Comprehension
  In second grade, your child will use his or her ability to read longer texts to greatly
  expand reading comprehension, or understanding the full meaning of what he
  or she reads. He or she will learn to recognize cause and effect relationships in
  different situations, draw conclusions, and infer information that is implied but not
  directly stated in a text. Your child will learn to read, write, and perform a series of
  events in sequential order. He or she will distinguish fiction and nonfiction and fact
  from opinion. As your child progresses, he or she will recognize important elements
  of a text such as the main idea, supporting details, characters, settings, and plots.

  To aid reading comprehension, take time to talk to your child about books he or she
  has read. Ask questions such as "What do you think the characters meant by…" or
  "Did that happen before or after…." After reading a good book, your child may
  have interest in doing a project based on what he or she learned. Some project
  ideas are making time lines, making new illustrations for the story, writing an
  alternate ending, or writing a letter to the author.

Language Skills

Language skills are often taught in the context of reading and writing. When you read together or look at your child's written work, take the opportunity to point out individual words, sentences, and punctuation marks on the page and talk about them. This will give your child a deeper understanding of how language works. Focus on the following topics:

- Spelling
  In second grade, your child will be encouraged to move away from "invented spelling" (or attempting to spell words the way they sound) toward "conventional spelling," which follows special rules and patterns. A first grader may be praised for spelling **luv**, but second graders will begin to learn that the correct spelling is **love**. Gently encourage your child to spell words correctly and point out interesting patterns in the spellings of words.

- Vocabulary Development
  During second grade, your child will study types of words such as nouns, pronouns, verbs, adjectives, adverbs, compound words (such as **sandbox**), contractions (such as **don't**), words with prefixes and suffixes added to a root word (such as **undo** and **trying**), synonyms (such as **pretty** and **beautiful**), and antonyms (such as **noisy** and **silent**). Make sure your child can provide an example of each type of word.

- Sentences
  Your child will learn to identify the subject and predicate of a sentence and combine two short sentences into one longer sentence. He or she will review types of sentences: statements, questions, exclamations, and commands. Your son or daughter will be encouraged to write complete sentences that begin with capital letters and end with punctuation marks.

Writing

As the year progresses, your child will be able to produce a piece of writing that stays on topic, includes supporting ideas, and has a beginning, middle, and end. Your child will write stories, fact-based reports, and pieces that give an opinion. Encourage your child to write frequently at home, experimenting with different formats such as traditional letters and notes, e-mails, illustrated stories, and diaries or journals. Keep a folder of your child's writing. From time to time, encourage your child to improve an old story or look over the year's work to celebrate his or her growth as a writer.

Second Grade Bound © Carson-Dellosa • CD-704635

Speaking and Listening

Good speaking and listening skills are essential to school success. By paying careful attention to what is being said, your child will not only learn more but will develop the skill of being a good conversationalist as well. Make sure to provide ample opportunities for your child to listen to songs, poetry, and stories.

Math

Math is everywhere in your child's world. Encourage your child to think about how math is used in daily activities such as helping in the kitchen, playing games, using blocks and other toys, and doing household chores. Let your child see that you use math every day, too, when you shop, pay bills, keep a calendar, or make home repairs. When helping with math, move from the concrete to the abstract. For example, help with subtraction first by modeling a problem with pennies or other small items, then by drawing pictures to show the problem, and finally by solving the problem with numbers on paper. Whenever possible, relate math concepts to your child's experiences. Focus on these second-grade math skills:

- Skip Counting
  Help your child begin with any number and count forward and backward by ones, twos, fives, and tens. Encourage your child to count while clapping, jumping rope, or doing other rhythmic activities.

- Addition and Subtraction Without Regrouping
  Make sure your child has mastered basic single-digit addition and subtraction facts. Flash cards are a good tool for developing speed and memorization. As your child advances to two- and three-digit problems, point out that these are quick and easy to do once basic math facts are memorized.

- Place Value
  Help your child understand that the digits in numbers represent quantities of ones, tens, and hundreds. A number such as **368** has eight ones, six tens, and three hundreds. Be creative in finding ways for your child to use manipulatives to represent place value. To show a ten, your child might use a graph paper cut-out of ten squares, ten stacked interlocking blocks, or ten craft sticks bound with a rubber band. Let your child use such materials to model a variety of numbers.

- Word Problems
  Your child will use addition and subtraction to solve word problems. You can help at home by inventing word problems that relate to your child's activities and interests.

- Study Shapes
  In second grade, your child will recognize and draw two-dimensional shapes. He or she will partition shapes into halves and thirds to begin to explore fractions.

- Working with Time and Money
  Your child will tell time using digital and analog clocks and will solve problems that involve money amounts. These skills are ideal for practice at home. Provide pretend money to use for "buying" things at home or let your child earn a small amount of money to spend at a yard sale or discount store. Look for analog clocks in stores and restaurants and compare the times they show to the time shown on digital devices such as your phone.

- Measurement
  This year, your child will measure length using inches, feet, and yards, as well as centimeters and meters. Provide a ruler and a meter stick for your child to use at home. Encourage him or her to estimate the length of objects in your home and then measure to test the prediction.

- Graphing
  Look for graphs to read with your child in nonfiction books, in print and online newspapers, and on Web sites. Point out bar graphs, line graphs, and pie graphs. Find a simple graph and ask your child to use the information shown to answer questions. It can be fun to make graphs to represent things that are important to your child. Can he or she make a graph to show the different kinds of toys in a collection?

Reading and Language Arts

As with every new school year, the work your child will encounter in second grade will be even more challenging. You can help your child prepare by helping him or her reinforce the major skill and subject areas he or she already knows. With this information fresh in your child's mind, he or she will be prepared to dive into new challenges.

In second grade, your child's reading and writing skills will grow considerably. He or she will probably be reading fluently by the end of the school year. To support your child's love of reading, provide your child with a variety of books at different reading levels and genres. Reading is one of the most important things you can do with your child. The more children read, the better they become at reading, which, in turn, makes it an enjoyable activity. Reading can enhance your child's social skills and open up new worlds!

As you work through this book, encourage your child to complete as much of each activity as possible and offer guidance as needed. This will give your child the confidence he or she needs to succeed in second grade and beyond!

This Reading and Language Arts section will cover important skills your child needs to know, including:

- ABC Order
- Consonants
- Vowels
- Syllables
- Compound Words
- Synonyms and Antonyms
- Similes
- Nouns, Verbs, and Adjectives
- Sentences
- Capitalization and Punctuation
- Comparative Adjectives

- Drawing Conclusions
- Fact and Opinion
- Following Directions
- Sequencing
- Classifying
- Cause and Effect
- Comprehension
- Main Idea
- Critical Thinking
- Writing

Food for Gregory

Print Gregory's food in ABC order. Then draw each meal on the plate.

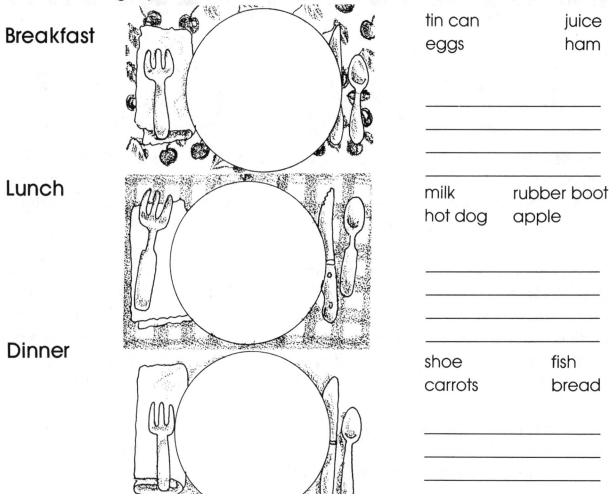

Breakfast

tin can   juice
eggs   ham

_____
_____
_____
_____

Lunch

milk   rubber boot
hot dog   apple

_____
_____
_____
_____

Dinner

shoe   fish
carrots   bread

_____
_____
_____
_____

Draw what you ate yesterday for breakfast, lunch and dinner on these plates.

Breakfast   **Lunch**   **Dinner**

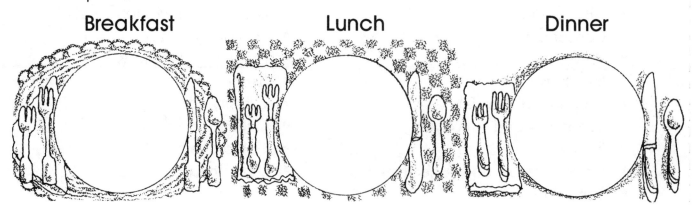

Which Part Shall I Play?

Grace loves to act out stories. Read the list of characters. Then write them in alphabetical order.

Joan of Arc
Anansi
Peter Pan
Juliet
Captain Hook
Hiawatha
Wendy
Romeo
Mowgli
Aladdin

1. _____

2. _____

3. _____

4. _____

5. _____

6. _____

7. _____

8. _____

9. _____

10. _____

Which Way?

Read the words in the Word Bank. Write them in alphabetical order on the lines.

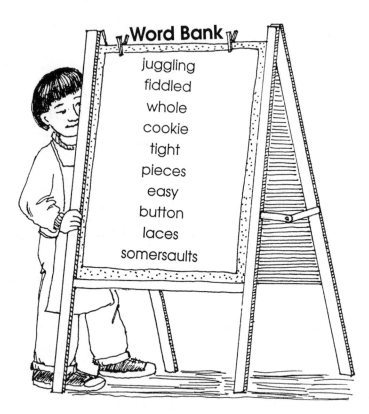

Word Bank

juggling
fiddled
whole
cookie
tight
pieces
easy
button
laces
somersaults

1. _____

2. _____

3. _____

4. _____

5. _____

6. _____

7. _____

8. _____

9. _____

10. _____

Write the missing lowercase letters in alphabetical order.

___ ___ c ___ ___ ___ ___ ___ h ___ ___ k ___ ___

___ o ___ ___ ___ ___ ___ u ___ ___ x ___ ___ ___

Second Grade Bound © Carson-Dellosa • CD-704635

ABC Potion

Write the words in alphabetical order.

1. _____
2. _____
3. _____
4. _____
5. _____
6. _____
7. _____
8. _____
9. _____
10. _____
11. _____
12. _____
13. _____
14. _____
15. _____

point
scientist
world
lightning
hard
baron
flashed
monster
rumbled
control
ketchup
overhead
drink
thunder
always

Crazy Creatures

Draw a line to each letter in ABC order to finish this dot-to-dot picture.

Now color and add details to the picture. Then write all the consonants in order on these lines.

1. _____ 5. _____ 9. _____ 13. _____ 17. _____ 21. _____

2. _____ 6. _____ 10. _____ 14. _____ 18. _____

3. _____ 7. _____ 11. _____ 15. _____ 19. _____

4. _____ 8. _____ 12. _____ 16. _____ 20. _____

Second Grade Bound © Carson-Dellosa • CD-704635

By Land, by Sea, and by Air

Write the first letter of the names of the objects below.
The letters form words.
Underline the word in **red** if it travels "By Land".
Underline the word in **green** if it travels "By Sea".
Underline the word in **orange** if it travels "By Air".

_____ _____ _____ _____ _____ _____

_____ _____ _____ _____ _____ _____ _____

_____ _____ _____ _____

_____ _____ _____ _____ _____ _____

Alphabet Soup

Nan Cook has a special way of making alphabet soup. She mixes two boxes of soup together. Then she adds two secret ingredients — mystery and fun. After the soup is cooked, a strange thing happens. All the vowels rise to the top of the pot.

Write the consonant that can be used in both the front and back of each vowel or pair of vowels to make a word. One is done for you.

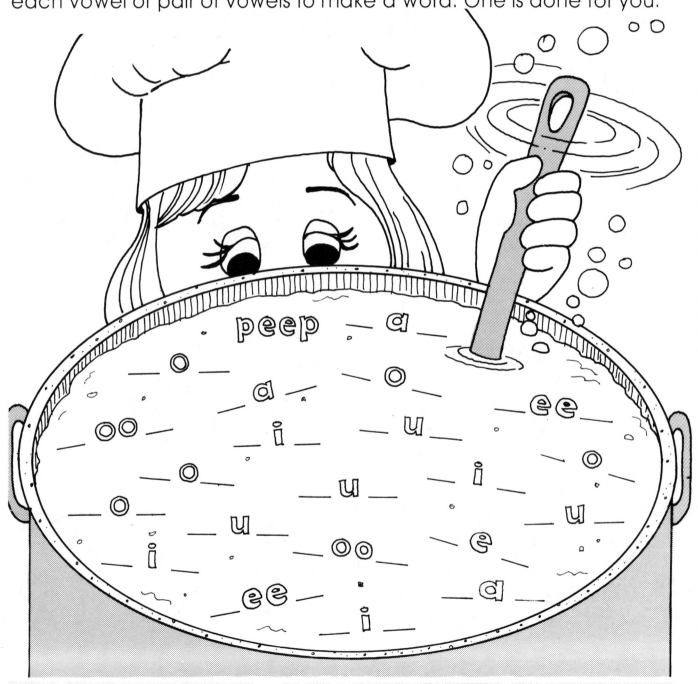

Stretch and Grow

Goofy Gladys got new glasses. The glasses had springs on them which stretched words out and then added another vowel to each one.

Add a vowel to each word below to see what words Gladys saw through her glasses.

1. pal   pa __ l

2. fed   fe __ d

3. chin   ch __ in

4. ran   ra __ n

5. cat   c __ at

6. Jon   jo __ n

7. shut   sh __ ut

8. bran   bra __ n

9. lid   l __ id

10. hat   h __ at

11. bad   b __ ad

12. flat   fl __ at

13. bit   b __ it

14. pin   p __ in

15. men   me __ n

Motorcycle Maze

Help Ralph move through the maze to the Mountain View Inn by tracing over the path in which all of the words have two syllables.

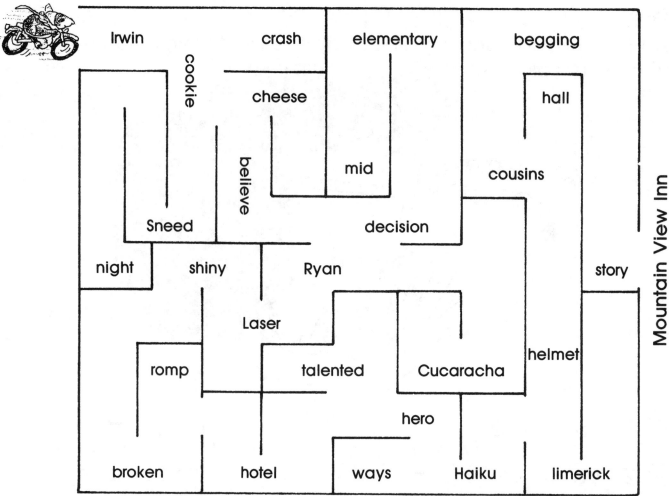

Now write the words from the correct path in alphabetical order on the lines below.

1. _____   8. _____
2. _____   9. _____
3. _____   10. _____
4. _____   11. _____
5. _____   12. _____
6. _____   13. _____
7. _____   14. _____

Trick or Treat Syllables

Think about how many syllables are in each word in the Word Bank. Then write each word on the correct jack-o'-lantern.

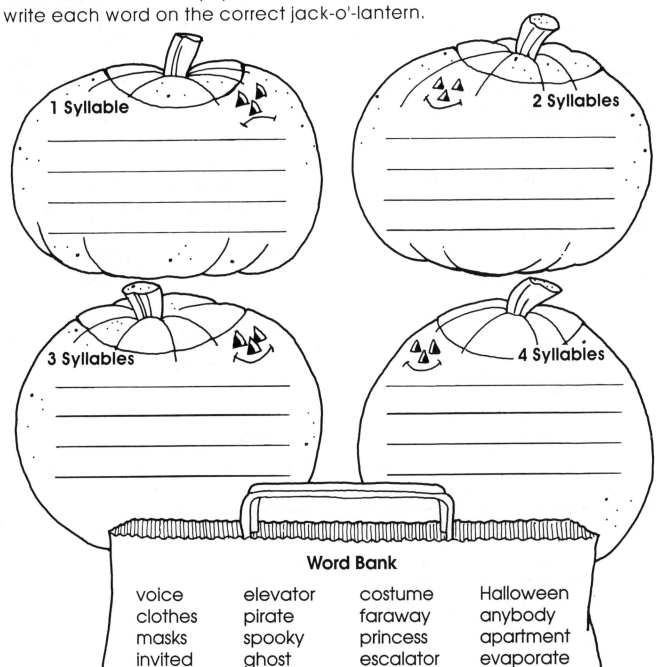

1 Syllable

2 Syllables

3 Syllables

4 Syllables

Word Bank

voice	elevator	costume	Halloween
clothes	pirate	faraway	anybody
masks	spooky	princess	apartment
invited	ghost	escalator	evaporate

Buddy's Lists

Buddy likes to make lists. Yesterday, he wrote a list of his favorite things to do with friends. Today, he wants to divide this list into three more lists. Help Buddy by filling in these three lists with one-syllable, two-syllable and three-syllable words from his word list. The first word has been done for you.

One-syllable words

1. golf
2. _____
3. _____
4. _____
5. _____

Buddy's Word List
Things to Do with Friends

golf   basketball
Ping-Pong™   camp
swim   snorkeling
backpacking   biking
volleyball   skate
baseball   canoeing
fishing   soccer
swing

Two-syllable words

1. _____
2. _____
3. _____
4. _____
5. _____

Three-syllable words

1. _____
2. _____
3. _____
4. _____
5. _____

All Together Now

Match a word in the Word Bank with a word on a feather to make a compound word. Then write it on the line.

space _____

cup _____

out _____

Thanks _____

with _____

on _____

news _____

your _____

some _____

Word Bank

back	out	paper	thing
fit	self	yard	cakes
man	giving	stage	school

Word Magic

Maggie Magician announced, "One plus one equals one!" The audience giggled. So Maggie put two words into a hat and waved her magic wand. When she reached into the hat, Maggie pulled out one word and a picture. "See," said Maggie, "I was right!"

Look at each picture below. Use the Word Bank to help write a compound word for each.

_____ _____ _____

_____ _____ _____

_____ _____ _____

_____ _____

Word Bank

ball	door	rain
basket	ear	shirt
bell	fish	shoe
book	foot	star
bow	lace	stool
box	light	sun
cake	mail	tail
cup	phone	worm

_____ _____

Compound Your Effort

Read each word. Find the word in the Word Bank that goes with it to make a compound word. Cross it out. Then write the compound word on the line.

1. coat _____

2. snow _____

3. home _____

4. waste _____

5. tip _____

6. chalk _____

7. note _____

8. grass _____

9. school _____

10. with _____

Look at the words in the Word Bank you did not use. Use those words to make your own compound words.

1. _____

2. _____

3. _____

4. _____

5. _____

Word Bank			
board	room	thing	side
writing	book	hopper	toe
bag	ball	class	where
work	out	basket	

Mystery Word Mix-Up

Put on your detective hat! How many words can you make using only the letters in the words:

N a t e   t h e   G r e a t

1. _____
2. _____
3. _____
4. _____
5. _____
6. _____
7. _____
8. _____
9. _____
10. _____
11. _____

12. _____
13. _____
14. _____
15. _____
16. _____
17. _____
18. _____
19. _____
20. _____
21. _____
22. _____

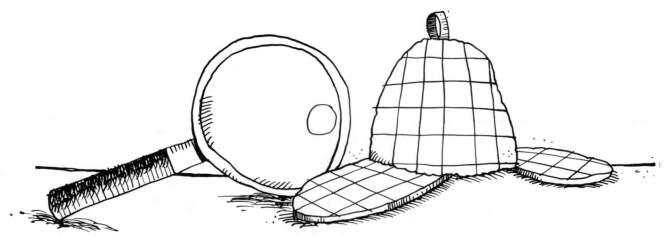

Flower Fun

Find words in the Word Bank that are synonyms for the words in the leaves.
Write them on the leaves.

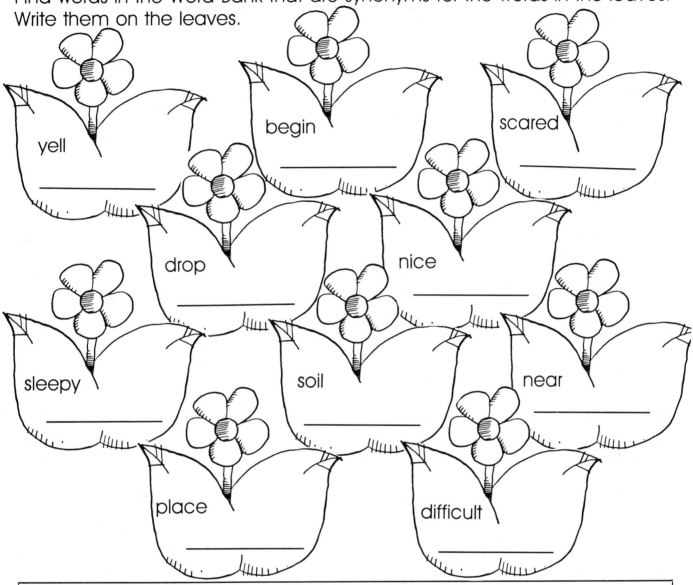

yell
_____

begin
_____

scared
_____

drop
_____

nice
_____

sleepy
_____

soil
_____

near
_____

place
_____

difficult
_____

Word Bank

pick	start	easy	sky
kind	rain	afraid	fall
close	hard	scream	awake
put	whisper	dirt	tired

Where?

Read each word on the left. Find its synonym in the Word Bank and write it on the line.

1. below   _____

2. drummed   _____

3. hear   _____

4. scrambled   _____

5. over   _____

6. close   _____

7. slipped   _____

8. woods   _____

9. spring   _____

10. cleaned   _____

11. sturdy   _____

12. paths   _____

13. perhaps   _____

14. house   _____

15. evening   _____

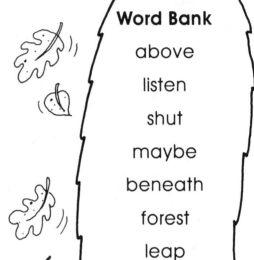

Word Bank

above
listen
shut
maybe
beneath
forest
leap
tapped
home
hurried
strong
sunset
trails
washed
slid

Who's Afraid?

Help Frog and Toad escape from the snake. Read the two words in each space. If the words are antonyms, color the space **green**. Do not color the other spaces.

go stop

large small

wide narrow

dinner supper

scared afraid

shut close

happy sad

fall rise

brave afraid

dark light

outside inside

higher lower

leap jump

tremble shake

fast quick

happy glad

look see

none all

top bottom

covers blankets

friend pal

stones rocks

down up

shout whisper

loud soft

under over

Toad's House

Should We Wake Them?

Read the words on each of the pillows. Find a word in the Word Bank that means the opposite and write it on the line.

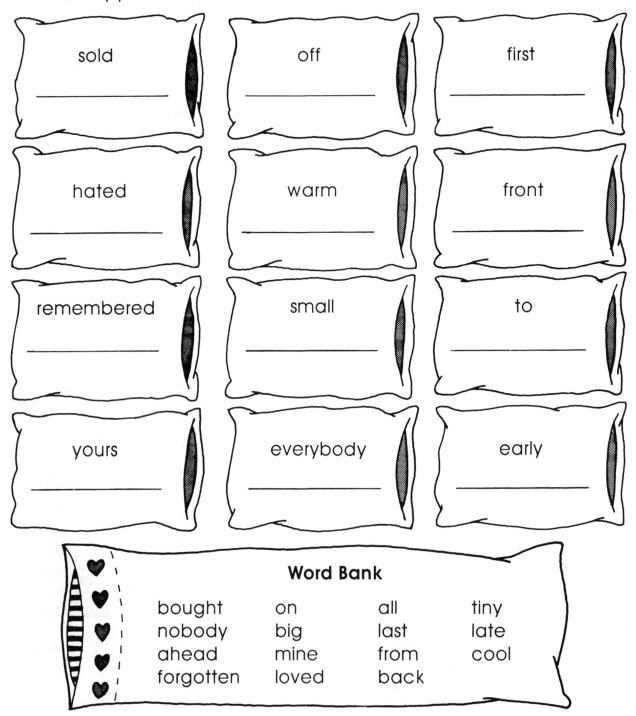

sold
_____

off
_____

first
_____

hated
_____

warm
_____

front
_____

remembered
_____

small
_____

to
_____

yours
_____

everybody
_____

early
_____

Word Bank

bought	on	all	tiny
nobody	big	last	late
ahead	mine	from	cool
forgotten	loved	back	

Flying Free Like An Eagle

Read the beginning of each sentence. Draw a line to the words on the feather that best complete each sentence.

1. The strong stallion fought like...

2. The bolt of lightning lit the sky like...

3. The wild horses roamed the hills as free as...

4. The thunder roared like...

5. The running herd crossed the land like...

6. The stallion's eyes were as cold as...

7. The hills were as dark as...

8. The rising sun was like...

the wind.

a wave rolling to shore.

a match being lit on a dark night.

a panther's coat.

a mighty warrior.

an arching rainbow.

an ice-covered pond.

an angry lion.

Rain, Rain Go Away!

Read the naming parts in the tent.
~~~🖊 one of the naming parts to begin each sentence.

Rain
Black clouds
A big wind
The campfire
Todd and Clint
The old green tent

1. _____ went camping.

2. _____ was hard to set up.

3. _____ blew the trees.

4. _____ filled the sky.

5. _____ ran off the tent.

6. _____ went out.

Name _____

Read the words in the Word Bank. If the word means **one**, write it on the paint jar. If the word means **more than one**, write it on the paintbrushes.

One

More than One

Word Bank

deed   people   berries   child   brushes

visions   paintbrush   boy   flowers

children   warrior   picture

Name _____

Fish for Plurals

Write the words on the fish in the correct tank.

| kites | mitten | star | cats | chick | matches | foxes | lunch |

One

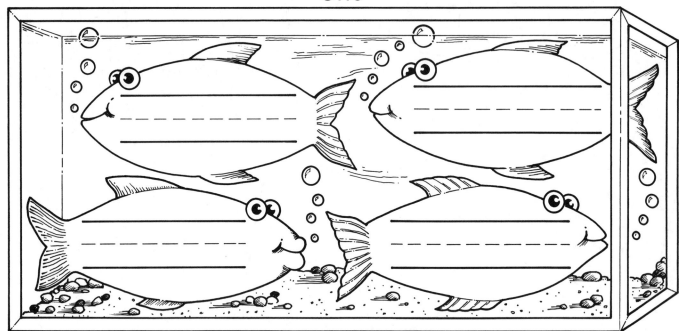

More Than One (Plural)

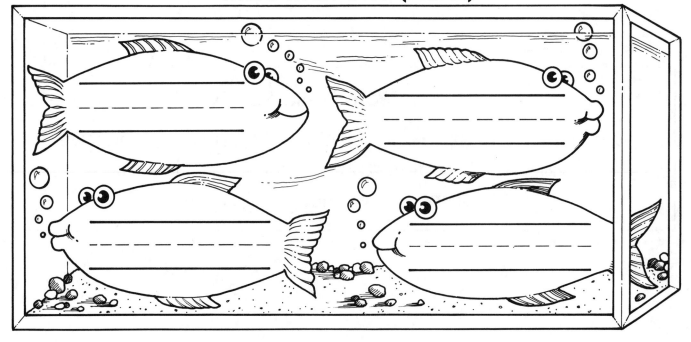

Fun Around the Campfire

Word Bank

beat	sang	told
clapped	sat	

a verb in each sentence below. Use the word bank to help you.

1. The boys and girls _____ around the campfire.

2. They _____ songs.

3. Brian _____ a drum.

4. Jenny and Helen _____ to the beat

5. The teacher _____ stories.

It's Time

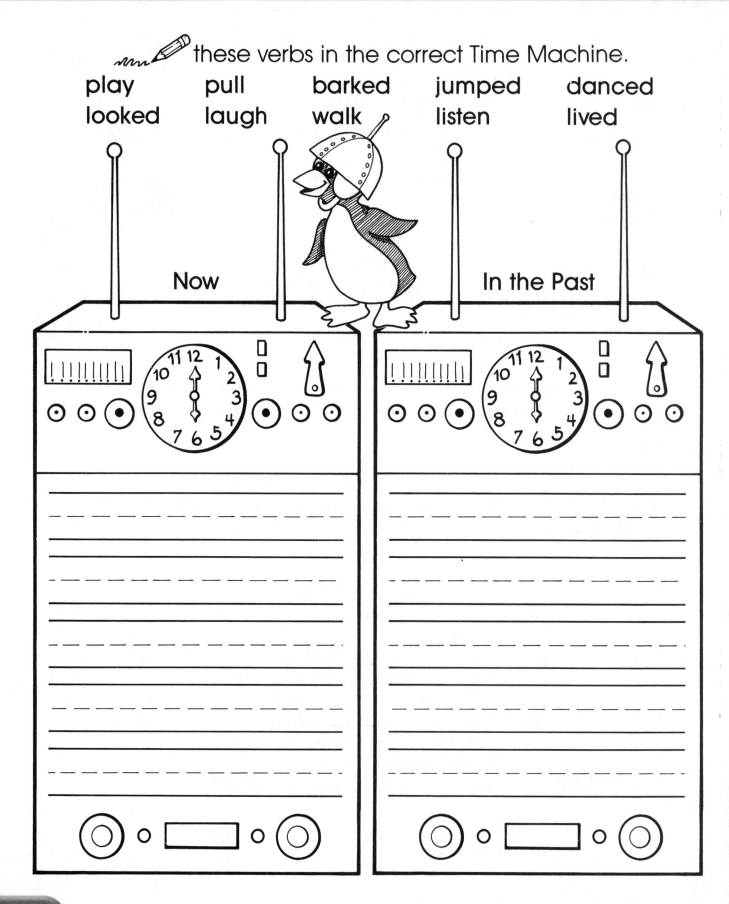

✎ these verbs in the correct Time Machine.

| play | pull | barked | jumped | danced |
| looked | laugh | walk | listen | lived |

Now

In the Past

Second Grade Bound © Carson-Dellosa • CD-704635

I Was. Were You?

Use "was" and "were" to tell about something that happened in the past. Use "was" to tell about one person or thing. Use "were" to tell about more than one person or thing. Always use "were" with the word "you."

✏️ "was" or "were" in each sentence below.

1. Lois _____ in the second grade last year.

2. She _____ eight years old.

3. Carmen and Judy _____ friends.

4. They _____ on the same soccer team.

5. I _____ on the team, too.

6. You _____ too young to play.

Playing in the Summer Sun

Look at the picture. Read the sentence. Circle the missing word. Then write it on the line.

It is _____
_____
_____.

rain   **raining**

He can _____
the boat. _____

row   **rowing**

The kite is _____
_____.

fly   **flying**

He is _____
_____.

swing   **swinging**

He is _____
_____.

pick   **picking**

An Owlish Activity

Write the words where they belong.

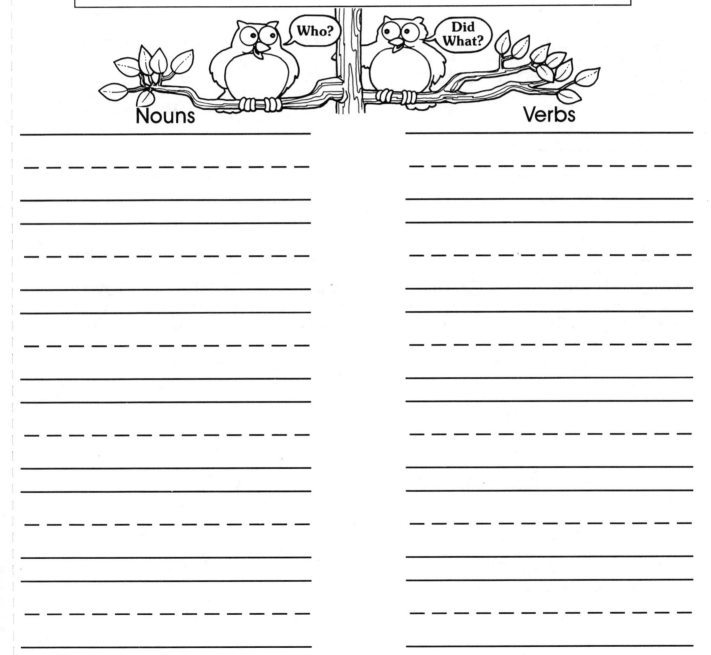

Word Bank

bite	school	children	skip	donkey	house
jump	lunchbox	kitten	write	hop	run

Nouns

Verbs

Tic-Tac-Toe

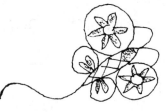

Circle all of the naming words (nouns).
Put an **X** on all of the doing words (verbs).
Under each game, write the **X** words that scored a tic-tac-toe.

boy	well	fell
mother	wished	ladder
ran	man	cake

_____

_____

fished	water	book
told	stone	lamp
pumped	people	shoe

_____

_____

child	sent	house
tree	ate	China
Chang	raced	body

_____

_____

paper	bear	bridge
Tikki	table	flower
read	yelled	jump

_____

_____

Picking Pronouns

The words *he, she, it,* and *they* can be used in place of a noun.

Read the sentence pairs. Write the correct pronoun in each blank.

1. John won first place.
   _____ got a blue ribbon.

2. Janet and Gail rode on a bus.
   _____ went to visit their grandmother.

3. Sarah had a birthday party.
   _____ invited six friends to the party.

4. The kitten likes to play.
   _____ likes to tug on shoelaces.

5. Ed is seven years old.
   _____ is in the second grade.

Marvelous Me!

You are a very special person!

Draw hair and eyes on the body below to make it look like you. Then use the describing words listed in the box to label your beautiful body parts. Be sure to label each part with a describing word that begins with the same letter. Tell a story about how each part of your body is special.

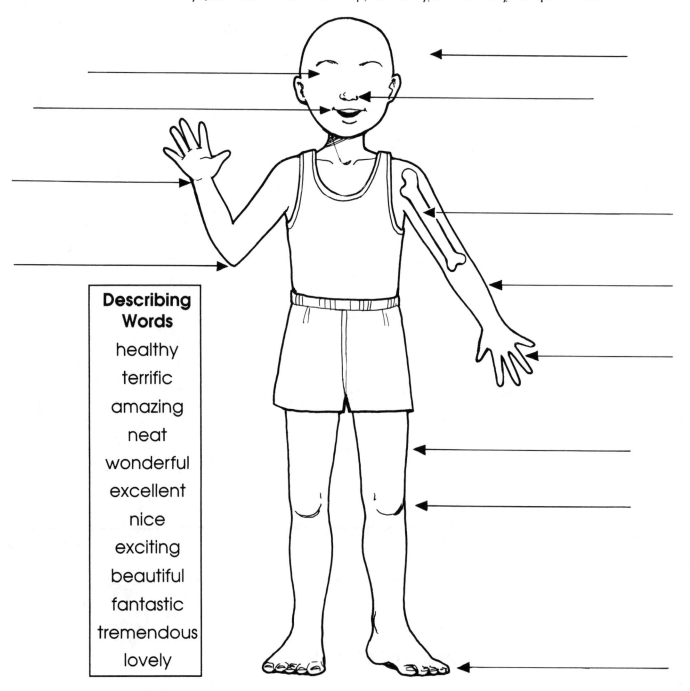

Describing Words

healthy

terrific

amazing

neat

wonderful

excellent

nice

exciting

beautiful

fantastic

tremendous

lovely

Add the Adjectives

Read each sentence. Write a describing word on each line. Draw a picture to match each sentence.

High
Mountain

The _____ flag waved over the _____ building.

A _____ lion searched for food in the _____ jungle.

We saw _____ fish in the _____ aquarium.

Her _____ car was parked by the _____ van.

The _____ dog barked and chased the _____ truck.

The _____ building was filled with _____ packages.

Wordy Treats

Write the word from the Word Bank on the correct trick or treat bag. If the word **names** a person, place or thing, write it on the bag marked **Nouns**. If the word **describes** something, write it on the bag marked **Adjectives**.

Nouns

1. _____
2. _____
3. _____
4. _____
5. _____
6. _____
7. _____
8. _____
9. _____

Adjectives

1. _____
2. _____
3. _____
4. _____
5. _____
6. _____
7. _____
8. _____
9. _____

Word Bank

costumes	elevator	pirate	fifth
ghosts	spooky	robot	bossy
party	squeaky	scary	stairs
special	wings	high	crown
	heavy	silly	

Summer Camp

A telling sentence begins with a capital letter and ends with a period. Write each telling sentence correctly on the lines.

1. everyone goes to breakfast at 6:30 each morning

   _____

2. only three people can ride in one canoe

   _____

3. each person must help clean the cabins

   _____

4. older campers should help younger campers

   _____

5. all lights are out by 9:00 each night

   _____

6. everyone should write home at least once a week

   _____

Tell-a-vision

Look at each TV picture. Write a telling sentence about each program.

_____

_____

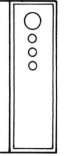

_____

_____

_____

_____

_____

_____

_____

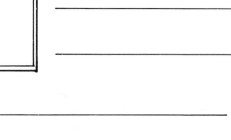

_____

_____

Second Grade Bound © Carson-Dellosa • CD-704635

Telephone Talk

An asking sentence is called a **question**. A question begins with a capital letter and ends with a question mark.

these questions correctly.

1. how old are you

_ _

2. are you in second grade

_ _

3. who is your teacher

_ _

4. did you read that book

_ _

5. where do you live

_ _

Asking Questions

Look at the picture. Write **five** asking sentences about the picture.

_____

_____

_____

_____

_____

That Doesn't Make Sense!

A sentence must make sense. Read each sentence. Put an **X** on the **two** words which do not belong. Write the corrected sentence on the lines below.

My neighbor is orange having a yard very sale.

1. _____

_____

She is snow selling lots of old things phone.

2. _____

_____

A man until is buying five candle old books.

3. _____

_____

My brother is buying an salt old checkers it game.

4. _____

_____

Two ladies pull are buying an old touch toy chest.

5. _____

_____

Flight to Fun

Would you like to fly away for a fun trip? Write words about a trip on the plane. Use the words to write five sentences about the trip.

1. _____

2. _____

3. _____

4. _____

5. _____

About Me

Sentences can tell much about you. Begin at the **START** sign and write sentences that tell all about you—how you look, your age, things you like to do, etc. Write as many sentences as you can going around and around the circle. Then draw a picture of yourself in the center of the circle.

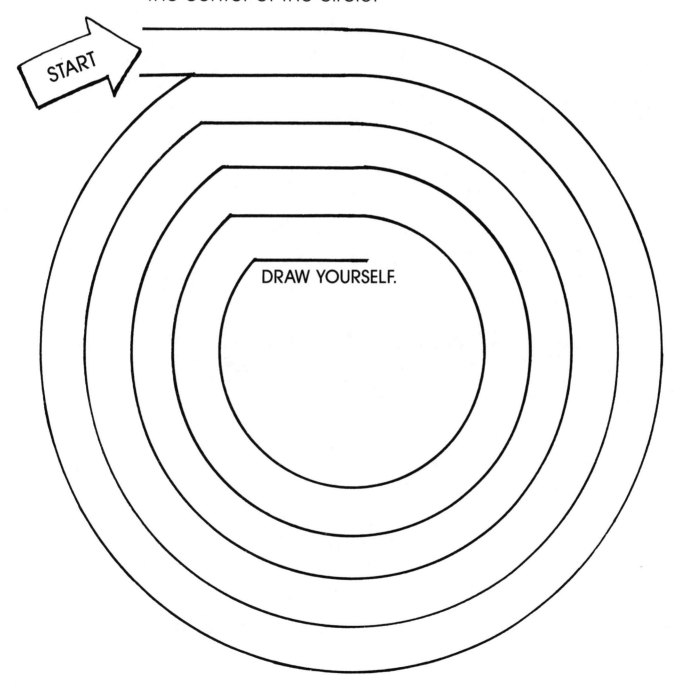

START

DRAW YOURSELF.

A Sensational Scent

Circle the letters that should be capital letters. Then write them in the matching numbered blanks to answer the question.

1. eddie, Homer's friend, lives on elm Street.
2. Homer's aunt lives in kansas City, kansas.
3. are you sure Aunt aggie is coming?
4. old Rip Van Winkle came to town.
5. The doughnuts were made by homer Price.
6. Miss terwillinger and Uncle telly saved yarn.
7. Homer Price was written by robert McCloskey.
8. Uncle ulysses owned a lunch room.
9. The super – Duper was a comic book hero.
10. Doc pelly lived in Homer's town.
11. money was stolen by the robbers.
12. now you have the answer to the question.

Who is hiding in the suitcase?

— — — — —   — — —   — — —   — — — — —
3 7 4 11 3   6 5 1   10 1 6   9 2 8 12 2

Now, How Does That Go?

Write the sentences correctly. Be sure to put capital letters, periods and exclamation marks where they belong.

1. muffy spoke the words very quietly

    _____

    _____

2. buster said that the pilgrims sailed on a ship named the mayflower

    _____

    _____

3. francine said, "i will not play the part of a turkey "

    _____

    _____

4. arthur thought about turkeys while he did dishes

    _____

    _____

5. arthur worried about finding a turkey

    _____

    _____

6. everyone looked at the audience and said, "happy thanksgiving "

    _____

    _____

Punctuation Magic

Write the sentences correctly. Be sure to put capital letters, periods and question marks where they belong.

1. mrs paris talked to richard, alex, matthew and emily about the trip to the museum

   _____

   _____

   _____

2. the children read a story about a king who was greedy

   _____

   _____

3. everyone but richard drew a picture about the story

   _____

   _____

4. why was drake sick

   _____

   _____

5. mrs gates asked matthew to take homework to drake

   _____

   _____

6. did richard's wish make drake sick

   _____

   _____

An Excellent Exercise

> The words **a** and **an** help point out a noun. Use **a** before a word that begins with a consonant. Use **an** before a word that begins with a vowel or a vowel sound.

1. Our class visited _____ farm.

2. We could only stay _____ hour.

3. A man let us pick eggs out of _____ nest.

4. We saw _____ egg that was cracked.

5. We watched _____ lady milk a cow.

6. We got to eat _____ ice cream cone.

Add an Apostrophe

> Add **'s** to a noun to show who or what owns something.

✏️ the correct word under each picture.

The ____ nose is big.
clown   clowns   clown's

This is ____ coat.
Bettys   Betty's   Betty

I know ____ brother.
Burt's   Burt   Burts

The ____ hat is pretty.
girls   girl   girl's

That is the ____ ball.
kitten's   kitten   kittens

My ____ shoe is missing.
sisters   sister   sister's

The ____ coach is Mr. Hall.
teams   team's   team

The ____ cover is torn.
book's   books   book

Who is Hungrier?

Use the pictures to help you complete each sentence with the correct word.

Sludge   **Fang**   **Big Hex**

sleepy sleepier sleepiest

1. Fang is _____ than Big Hex.
2. Big Hex is _____.
3. Sludge is the _____ of all.

 Rosamond **Annie** **Eric**

dirty dirtier dirtiest

1. Rosamond's shirt is the _____ of all.
2. Eric's shirt is _____ than Annie's.
3. Annie's shirt is _____.

 Marshmallow **cotton ball** **pillow**

soft softer softest

1. The pillow is _____.
2. The cotton ball is the _____ of all.
3. The marshmallow is _____ than the pillow.

 Nate **Finley** **Pip**

hungry hungrier hungriest

1. Pip is _____ than Nate.
2. Nate is _____.
3. Finley is the _____ of all.

Read each sentence. Choose the correct word and write it on the line.

big
bigger
biggest

1. The town made the _____ snowball on record.
2. Emmett made a _____ snowball.
3. Sara helped him make it even _____ .

fast
faster
fastest

1. The snowball started to roll very _____ .
2. It was the _____ rolling snowball anyone had ever seen.
3. It rolled _____ than they could run.

white
whiter
whitest

1. Mr. Wetzel's face turned _____ when he saw the snowballrolling toward his candy store.
2. As the snowball rolled closer, Mr. Wetzel's face became even _____ .
3. After it snowed all night, the town was the _____ it had ever been.

Bunny Bunch

There are ten bunnies in this family. Each one is special.

Read the clues and fill in the blank with the word that rhymes and makes sense.

1. I like to hop
   and drink _____ .

2. I can run fast,
   but still I am always _____ .

3. I like to run and jump,
   but sometimes I fall and get a _____ .

4. I like to help Mom and Pop
   by scrubbing the floor with a _____ .

5. After I feed the cat,
   I take out my baseball and _____ .

6. I like to go on a hike
   or ride my _____ .

7. I like to dig in the sand
   and play the drums in a _____ .

8. I like to play with a toy car
   while I eat a candy _____ .

9. I can walk in the fog
   and also chop a _____ .

10. I can fly my kite
    but not during the _____ .

band
bar
bat
bike
bump
cast
daylight
far
fat
fog
hand
last
like
log
mop
night
pop
pump
stop
top

Loosey Goosey

Find the names of the birds at the bottom of the page that will rhyme with the words given. For example: Loose goose

narrow _____

hairy _____

men _____

pork _____

love _____

pleasant _____

perky _____

soon _____

luck _____

darling _____

bobbin _____

dark _____

pinch _____

muffin _____

beagle _____

frail _____

hull _____

lay _____

howl _____

dove
stork
canary
wren
robin
jay

starling
sparrow
pheasant
eagle
turkey
owl
gull

quail
loon
puffin
duck
lark
finch

Do You Know a Boa?

Print a rhyming word under each word on the boa's body. Slither down from the head to the tail.

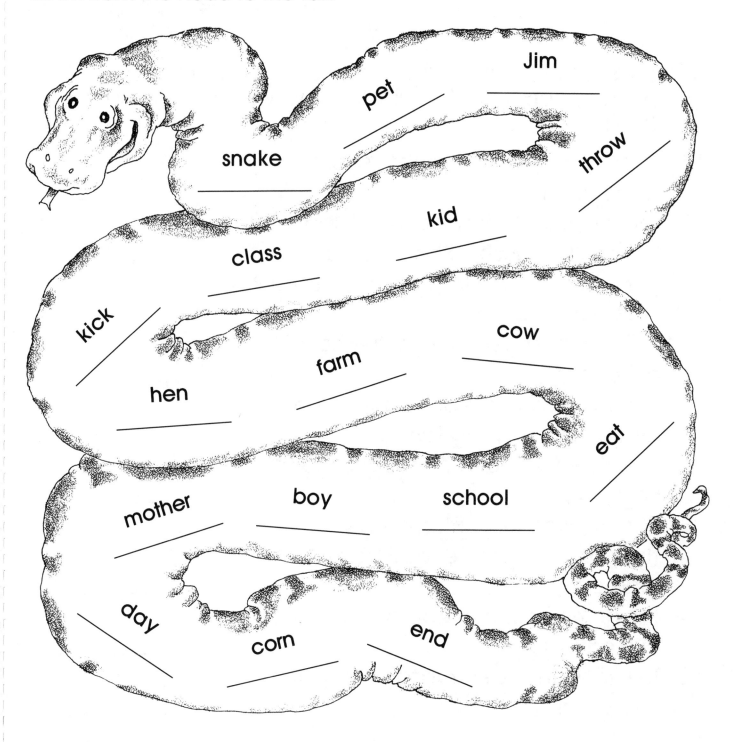

High-Flying Acts

Read each sentence. Look at the underlined words. Write **who, what, when, where** or **why** to show what the underlined words tell.

1. Clifford and Emily Elizabeth spent the day <u>at the circus</u>. _____

2. The biggest elephant couldn't lead the parade <u>because he had a cold</u>. _____

3. <u>The circus owner</u> was afraid there would not be a show. _____

4. Clifford shot <u>a tent pole</u> at the hot air balloon. _____

5. Clifford caught the diver <u>before he landed in the empty tank</u>. _____

6. The clowns needed help <u>because some had quit</u>. _____

7. Clifford liked <u>the cotton candy</u>. _____

8. The poster said there would be a circus <u>today</u>. _____

9. The human cannon ball landed <u>on top of a haystack</u>. _____

10. The lions and tigers didn't listen to <u>the lion tamer</u>. _____

Donuts, Anyone?

WANNA BUY a DONUT?

Write **who**, **what**, **when**, **where** or **why** to show what the underlined words in each sentence tell you.

1. The Pee Wee Scouts went to <u>Mrs. Peter's house</u> on Tuesday.   _____

2. <u>The Scouts</u> turned in the money they had received for selling the boxes of donuts.   _____

3. Roger and Rachel sold the most <u>boxes of donuts.</u>   _____

4. Sonny's mother sold many boxes <u>at work.</u>   _____

5. Rachel sold the donuts to <u>her relatives.</u>   _____

6. Rachel was angry at Molly <u>because she was making fun of her relatives.</u>   _____

7. Sonny and Rachel would win badges <u>because they sold the most boxes of donuts.</u>   _____

8. If people eat <u>a lot of donuts,</u> they might get fat.   _____

9. Everyone was happy that they had earned enough money to go to camp <u>in two weeks.</u>   _____

10. The Scout meeting started <u>after three o'clock.</u>   _____

It's a Surprise!

Read the clues. Find the answers in the Word Bank.

1. You need snow to do this. You can go fast or slow. You can turn corners. You need a pair of something to do this. What is it?

_____

2. This can be soft or hard. It can be made of paper or metal. You need it when you want to buy something. What is it?

_____

3. It is a place where you can buy sweet treats to eat. Many of the treats that can be bought there have to be baked in an oven. What is it?

_____

4. In larger cities these come out every day. It can have a few pages or many pages. It tells you what is happening in the world. What is it?

_____

5. It can be large or small. It smells very good. It is green. People like to decorate it at one time of the year. What is it?

_____

6. It needs gas. It is very big. Its driver stops a lot at people's houses to pick up things. What is it?

_____

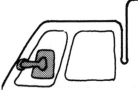

Word Bank

book	magazine	newspaper	garbage truck
coins	paper bag	holly plant	Christmas tree
money	gas station	candy store	snowballing
skiing	sledding	bakery	

Reflect on the Riddles

Read each riddle. Find the answer in the Word Bank and write it on the line.

1. There are two of me. We can blink. We can see. We can wink. We can weep.

   What are we? _____

2. There is one of me. I can sing. I can form words. I can eat. I can even blow a big bubble. I can eat ice cream, too.

   What am I? _____

3. There is one of me. If I tickle, I will sneeze. I like to sniff flowers. I like the whiff of hot dogs, also.

   What am I? _____

4. We need to bend and stretch. We need rest. We need to work and we need to play. We are all different.

   What are we? _____

5. I can be almost any color. I can be long or short. I can be curled and I can be spiked.

   What am I? _____

6. We can change. We can be happy or sad. We can be worried or excited. We can even be scared.

   What are we? _____

7. I cover a lot. I keep muscles, bones, and blood inside your body. I let you know if it is hot or cold. I tell you if something is wet or dry.

   What am I? _____

8. We all have feelings. We all have bodies. We all like to do many of the same things. But, we also are all very different.

   Who are we? _____

Word Bank

bodies	eyes
people	feelings
hair	mouth
nose	skin

The Adventure Begins

One rainy Saturday morning, Patrick, Brenda, and Jamie decided they needed something new and exciting to do that morning. They took out the telephone book and turned to the yellow pages. In it they found these advertisements for special places to visit.

Aquarium

Open weekdays from
10:00 a.m. to 6:00 p.m.
Closed weekends

Call 123 - Fish

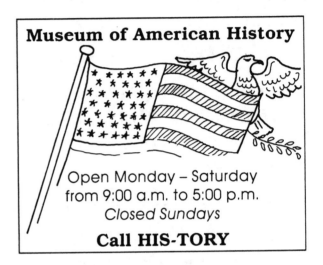

Museum of American History

Open Monday – Saturday
from 9:00 a.m. to 5:00 p.m.
Closed Sundays

Call HIS-TORY

Planetarium

Open Mon. – Friday
12:00 noon to 6:00 p.m.
Saturday 3:00 p.m. to 9:00 p.m.

Call 83S - TARS

Zoo

Open daily from
9:00 a.m. to 5:00 p.m.
Weather Permitting

Call ANI - MALS

The children looked carefully at the ads. Which place did they choose to visit and why?

They chose to go to the _____

because _____

It's a Fact!

Read each sentence. If it states a fact, write the word **fact** on the line. If it states an opinion, write the word **opinion** on the line.

1. An opera is a play that is sung. _____

2. Many operas are terribly boring. _____

3. Opera stars wear costumes on stage. _____

4. People who have trunks filled with jewels are robbers. _____

5. In many cities people dial 911 for emergency help. _____

6. It is fun to check the mailbox every day. _____

7. Seventy is a very old age. _____

8. Second and third grade are about the same. _____

9. Many operas are recorded on records. _____

10. It is all right to snoop in other people's things if you have a reason. _____

Is This for Real?

Read each sentence. If it tells something that could really happen, draw a pumpkin on the line.

1. Spiders spin cobwebs. _____

2. Robots are people. _____

3. Cats have nine lives. _____

4. Bats hang upside down. _____

5. Ghosts haunt houses. _____

6. There really are spooks. _____

7. A mask can hide your face. _____

8. Boys and girls can run in high heels. _____

9. Owls have wings. _____

10. Witches ride on brooms. _____

11. Some people buy costumes. _____

12. Pirates sail on ships. _____

Second Grade Bound © Carson-Dellosa • CD-704635

Top, Middle, Bottom

Read and follow the directions.

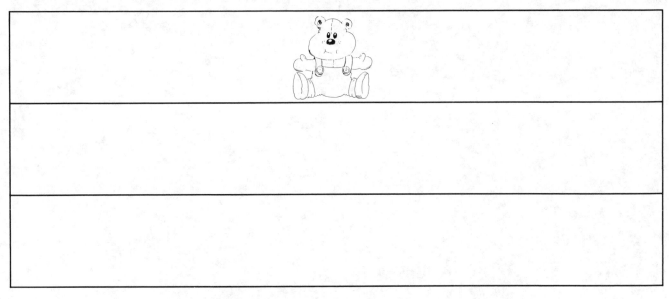

1. Paste the dog in the middle of the bottom shelf.
2. Paste the cat on the right side of the bear.
3. Paste the rabbit on the left side of the top shelf.
4. Paste the elephant on the shelf below the rabbit.
5. Paste the frog on the left side of the bottom shelf.
6. Paste the horse on the middle shelf below the cat.
7. Paste the giraffe on the middle shelf above the dog.
8. Paste the turtle on the right side of the bottom shelf.

Cut _

Where Is It?

Follow the directions. **Hint:** Read through all of the directions before starting.

1. Draw a brown mound in the middle of the box.
2. Draw a red car on top of the mound.
3. Draw apartments behind and to the left of the mound.
4. Draw a bird nest, with four blue eggs inside, on top of the car.
5. Draw three yellow birds flying away from the nest.
6. Draw two tin cans at the bottom of the mound.
7. Put an **X** on one of the tin cans.
8. Draw you and your friend looking at the car.

I'll Try Another Way

Help the little mole find his way to Percy's hut. Read and follow the directions. Write each word that tells what blocks his path as he looks for the loose floorboard. Then draw a line to show where the mole traveled.

						brick	
			rock				
	pipe						
				puddle of water			
			log				floor-board

Go right 1 space, then down 1 space. There is a _____ .

Go left 1 space, down 3 spaces,
then right 2 spaces. There is a _____ .

Go up 1 space, right 1 space, then up 1. There is a _____ .

Go left 1 space, up 2, then right 3 spaces. There is a _____ .

Go down 1 space, right 2 spaces,
down 2, then left 2 spaces. There is a _____ .

Go down 1 space, then right 1 space. Hooray! It's the _____ .

Build a Community

Cut out the pictures at the bottom of this page. Read the directions. Paste the pictures where they belong.

1. Place the school **west** of the house and **east** of the row of trees.
2. Place the train at the **southwest** edge of the railroad tracks.
3. Place the Police Station **west** of the Train Station and **east** of the train.
4. Place the Grocery Store **east** of the house and **south** of the rising sun.
5. Place the Bank **north** of the train.
6. Place the Firehouse **south** of the Grocery Store and **east** of the Train Station.

Cut ✂ ╌╌╌╌╌╌╌╌╌╌╌╌╌╌╌╌╌╌╌╌╌╌╌╌╌╌╌╌╌╌╌

Just Being Neighborly

Go along with Percival Porcupine as he delivers the Welcome basket.

Follow the directions. Trace a path from one place to the next.

1. Start at Percival and go east 3 spaces. Write **library.**
2. Then go south 4 spaces. Write **market**.
3. Next go west 2 spaces. Write **gas station**.
4. Now go north 3 spaces. Write **school**.
5. Go west 2 spaces. Write **fire station**.
6. Go south 2 spaces. Write **park**.
7. Go east 6 spaces. Write **welcome**.

Plotting Plants

Follow Rupert Rabbit as he learns about plants. Use the words in the Word Bank to help you.

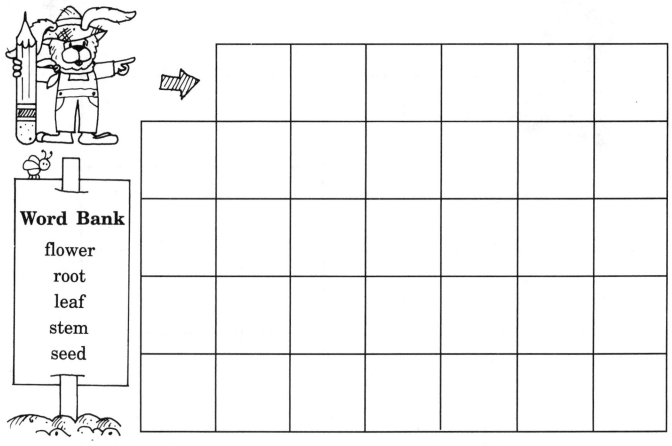

Word Bank

flower
root
leaf
stem
seed

Read and follow the directions. Start at Rupert Rabbit.

1. Go right 5 spaces. Then go down 3 spaces and left 5 spaces. Write the word that names what grows into a new plant here.

2. Now go up 2 spaces. Then go right 6 spaces and down 3 spaces. Write the word that names the part of the plant that is underground here.

3. Now go up 3 spaces. Then go left 3 spaces and down 1 space. Write the word that names the part of the plant that makes the food here.

4. Now go right 2 spaces. Then go up 1 space and left 4 spaces. Write the word that names the part of the plant that carries food and water to the rest of the plant here.

5. Now go down 2 spaces. Then go right 5 spaces and up 3 spaces. Write the word that names the part of the plant that makes the seeds here.

What Did I Say?

Unscramble the words in each 💬 . ✏️ each sentence on the line.

The One in the Middle

Print the words in order to make a sentence. The word in the middle is there to help you. Print the sentences.

1. good   Dissel   jumper   Freddy   a
    _____ was _____

2. was   Gumber   teacher   Ms.
    _____ Freddy's _____

3. and   one   sister   had   Freddy   one
    _____ brother _____

4. Freddy   play   going   in   was   to   a
    _____ be _____

5. green   They   face   on   painted   his
    _____ dots _____

6. break   Gumber   to   a   told   leg   Ms.
    _____ Freddy _____

Now color this picture.

What Do I Do First?

Look at the pictures. Number them in the correct order. Then read and number the sentences in the correct order.

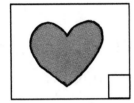 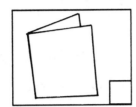 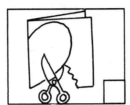 

___ Cut along the line.

___ Fold a piece of paper in half.

___ Draw one half of a heart on the paper.

___ Open the heart.

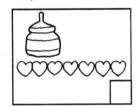 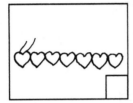 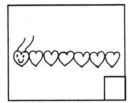 

___ Draw two antennae on the first heart.

___ Paste the hearts in a line.

___ Then draw two eyes and a mouth on the first heart.

___ Cut out seven small hearts.

What did you make? _____

 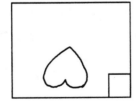 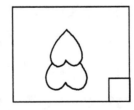 

___ Draw two eyes and a nose. Paste a cotton ball on the big heart.

___ Paste a big heart upside down on a piece of paper.

___ Glue a smaller heart upside down on top of the big heart.

___ Paste two long skinny hearts upside down on the smaller heart.

What did you make? _____

Terrific Toast

Lionel said he made the best toast in the world! Number the sentences to show the best order to make terrific toast. The first two are done.

____ Close the jar of jam.

____ Close the package of bread.

____ Push down on the toaster button.

____ Put butter on the hot toast.

____ Place the plate of toast on the table and enjoy.

_2_ Open the package of bread.

_1_ Plug in the toaster.

____ Put the toast on a plate.

____ Take out two slices of bread.

____ Place the two slices of bread in the toaster.

____ Open the jar of jam.

____ Wait for the toast to pop up.

____ Put jam on the toast.

____ Take the toast out of the toaster.

What do you like to put on your toast? _____

_____

What is your favorite flavor of jam? _____

What's What?

Write the words from the Word Bank in the correct category.

Living	Non-Living
1. _____	1. _____
2. _____	2. _____
3. _____	3. _____
4. _____	4. _____
5. _____	5. _____
6. _____	6. _____

Word Bank

car	kitten	cow
truck	nest	plane
hen	boat	dog
bird	rocks	tree

Tidying Up

Write the words from the Word Bank in the correct category.

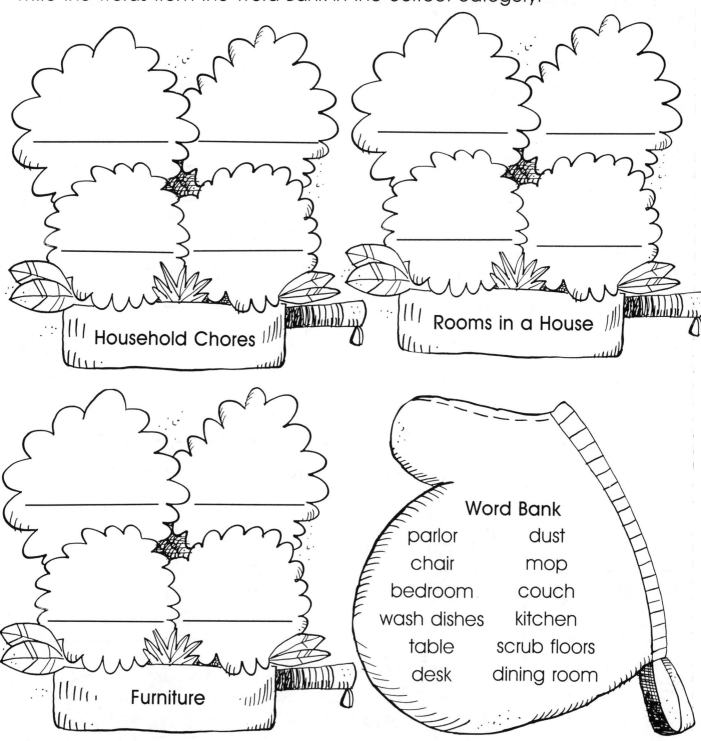

Household Chores

Rooms in a House

Furniture

Word Bank

parlor	dust
chair	mop
bedroom	couch
wash dishes	kitchen
table	scrub floors
desk	dining room

Cookie Jar

Read the categories on the jars. Cut and paste the cookies in the correct jar.

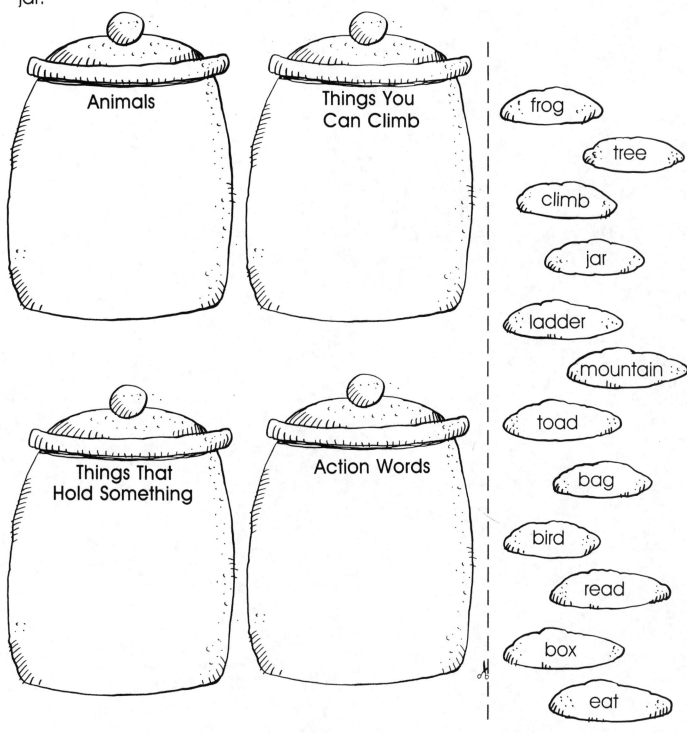

Sense-sational!

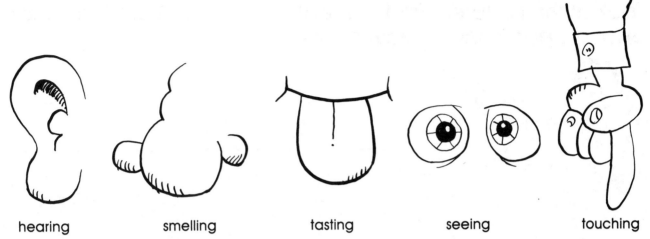

| hearing | smelling | tasting | seeing | touching |

Read each sentence. Then write which sense would be used for each one.

1. Andrew found page 64 in his reading book. _____

2. Andrew heard Sharon giggling at him. _____

3. Andrew poked Nicky. _____

4. Sharon was listening when Andrew asked Nicky about his freckles. _____

5. Andrew liked to count Nicky's freckles. _____

6. The number of freckles you get depends on how much of the juice you drink. _____

7. The bell rang and the students lined up. _____

8. Andrew couldn't find any freckles on Sharon's face. _____

9. Sharon ate bugs. _____

10. Miss Kelly told Andrew that it was time for his reading group. _____

What's Going On?

Look at the pictures. Find the sentence in the Word Bank that explains each one. Write it on the lines.

_____
_____

_____
_____

_____
_____

_____
_____

Word Bank

The team was treated to hot dogs after their win.

They won the big Thanksgiving game.

Coach Swamp made them practice hard.

The team had lost every game.

Lacy Patterns

Kim likes to look at the lacy patterns of snowflakes with her magnifying glass. Most of them have six sides or six points. But she has never seen two snowflakes that are alike. Kim catches them on small pieces of dark paper so that she can see them better. Some of the snowflakes are broken because they bump into each other as they fall from the clouds.

Color.

What does Kim use to make the snowflakes look bigger?

Check.

Most snowflakes have ☐ seven ☐ six ☐ five   sides or points.

Kim looks at them on dark pieces of paper so that she can...

☐ take them to school.   ☐ make a picture.   ☐ see them better.

Write.

Why are some of the snowflakes broken?

_____

- -

_____

- Finish the snowflake.

Faraway and Close Up

Kim's favorite subject is science. She has a telescope and a microscope in her bedroom. At night, she looks through her telescope. Things that are far away, like the moon, stars and planets, look bigger. When she looks through her microscope, she can see tiny things close up, like a drop of water or a bit of salt.

Unscramble and write.

_____

. _ _ _ _ _ _ _

Kim's favorite subject is _____.

niecsec

Circle.

She has a   bicycle   and a   microscope   in her bedroom.
            telescope   planet

Color.

What faraway things look bigger with a telescope?

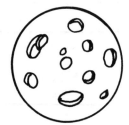   

Check.

When Kim looks through her microscope, she can see ...

☐ tiny things close up.   ☐ big things far away.

Second Grade Bound © Carson-Dellosa • CD-704635

Planets

There are eight planets that move around the sun. Our planet is Earth. Earth is closest to Mars and Venus. Jupiter is the largest planet. It is many times larger than Earth. Saturn is the planet with seven rings around it. The smallest planet is called Mercury!

Circle.

How many planets are there?   three   eight   seven

| Mercury | Earth | Jupiter | Mars | Venus | Saturn |

Write.

_____ I am your planet.

_____ } We are closest to Earth.

_____ I am the largest planet.

_____ I am the planet with seven rings.

_____ I am the smallest planet.

Color.
Draw three red rings around Saturn.

• Draw what you think you would find on the planet Mercury.

The Subway

Some big cities have a subway. A subway is a railroad that is under the ground. The trains carry people from one part of the city to another. The trains stop often to let people off and on. Many people ride to work on a subway. Others ride to school or to go shopping. Subways are nice because they do not take up space in a city.

Write.

A _____ is a railroad that is under the ground.

      shop   subway

Circle.

Yes or No

The subway takes people to parts of the city.	Yes	No
The subway stops only one time each day.	Yes	No
The subway stops to let people off and on.	Yes	No

Circle.

Where are some people on the subway going?

work   sleep   school   shopping

Color the subway train **red**.

• Draw where **you** would go on the subway.

A Helicopter

Would you like to ride in a helicopter? A helicopter flies in the air. It can fly **up** and **down**. It can fly **forward** and **backward**. It can fly **sideways**. A helicopter can even stay in one spot in the air! Helicopters can be many sizes. Some helicopters carry just one person. Some carry 30 people. Helicopters can be used for many jobs.

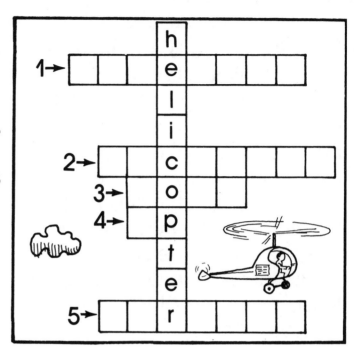

Write.

A _____ flies in the air.

　　　　trailer　　　　helicopter

Write.

Which way can a helicopter fly? (Look at story.)

4→u __   3→d __ __ __   5→f __ __ __ __ __ __ __

2→b __ __ __ __ __ __ __   1→s __ __ __ __ __ __ __

Write the answers in the puzzle above.

Circle.

Yes or No

A helicopter can stay in one spot in the air.　　　Yes　　No

Helicopters come in many sizes.　　　Yes　　No

All helicopters can carry 10 people.　　　Yes　　No

• Draw a big green helicopter.

Hot Air Balloons

Would you like to fly in a hot air balloon? A hot air balloon can fly when it is filled with hot air or a gas, called helium. Most hot air balloons use helium to fly. People can ride in a basket that is tied to the balloon. The wind moves the balloon in the sky. To come down, the people must let some of the air or gas out of the balloon.

Circle.
What does a hot air balloon need to fly?

        hot air   music   gas

Write.
Most hot air balloons use _____ to fly.

                helmets   helium

Circle.
What do people ride in?

cart    basket

Circle.

The   moon   moves the balloon in the sky.
        wind

Color.
1 - red   **2** - purple   **3** - green

• Draw a hot air balloon with two people in the basket.

What an Act!

Read about each act. Read the titles in the Word Bank. Write the best title for each act.

1. The lady climbed on the horse's back. The horse galloped around the ring as she stood up on its back.

   _____

2. Four seals stood up on their flippers. They spun and tossed a ball to each other. The biggest seal threw it to his trainer, Mac, who threw it back.

   _____

3. The trainer led the five bears into the ring. Each bear had its own bike. They rode up and down ramps as they raced each other around the ring.

   _____

4. The clowns tumbled as they came into the ring. They did forward rolls, backward rolls and even walked on their hands.

   _____

Word Bank

Three Brown Bears
Mac and His Ball-Playing Seals
A Horse Rider
The Tumbling Clowns

Mac and His Seals
The Bike-Riding Bears
Lady on a Galloping Horse
The Lazy Clowns

Can I or Can't I?

Read each sentence. Write **can** or **can't** on the line.

_____
_ _ _ _ _ _ _ _

1. The day is warm so I _____ wear my mittens.

_____
_ _ _ _ _ _ _ _

2. It is snowing so I _____ wear my snowsuit.

_____
_ _ _ _ _ _ _ _

3. My boots are too big so I _____ wear them.

_____
_ _ _ _ _ _ _ _

4. My hat is too little so I _____ wear it.

_____
_ _ _ _ _ _ _ _

5. It snowed so I _____ make a snowman.

_____
_ _ _ _ _ _ _ _

6. The shade will not open so I _____ see if it has snowed.

Just Rolling Along!

Help Emmett roll the snowball down the hill. Read the clues. Then find the words in the Word Bank and write them in the correct spaces. **Hint:** The last letter of each answer is the first letter of the next answer.

1. Boasting
2. Very, very good
3. Many moving cars and trucks
4. A little cold
5. Paid attention
6. Twice an amount
7. Comes after seventh
8. One of two equal parts
9. Very well-known
10. Not crooked

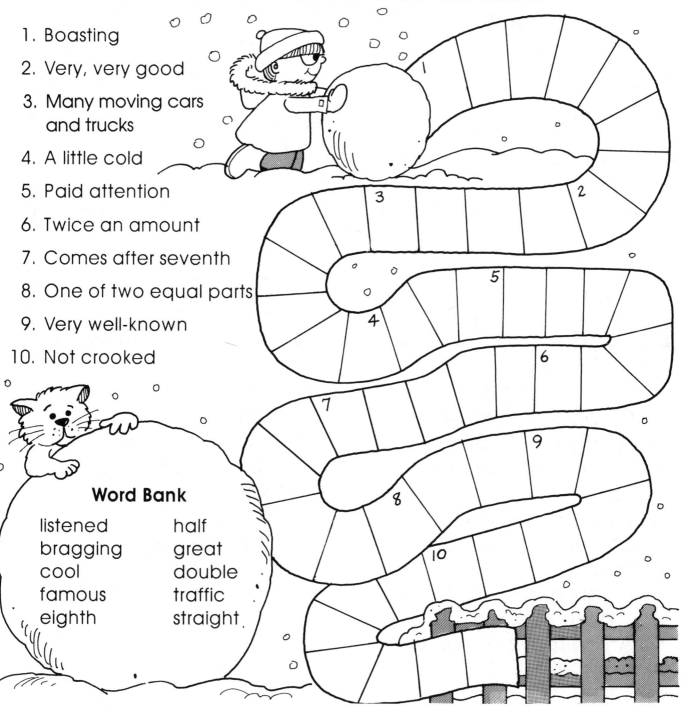

Word Bank

listened	half
bragging	great
cool	double
famous	traffic
eighth	straight

A-maze-ing

Draw a line through the maze in the order of the clues to help baby bird find his way back to his nest.

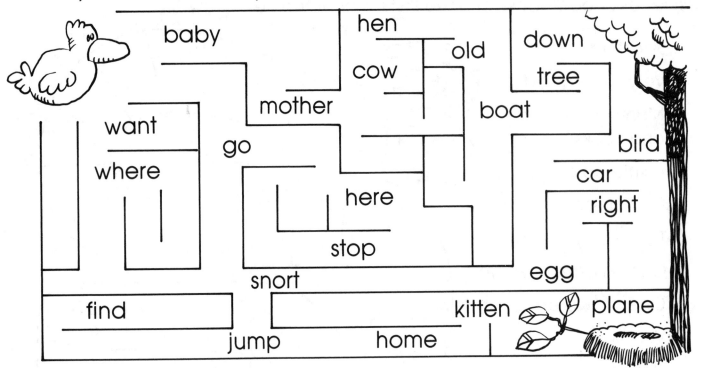

Clues

1. A very young child
2. Opposite of **father**
3. A large farm animal
4. A bird that lives on a farm
5. Opposite of **new**
6. Something that can float
7. A very large plant
8. Opposite of **up**
9. An animal that can fly
10. Something you can drive
11. Opposite of **left**
12. A bird hatches out of it
13. A sound
14. To leap
15. Your house
16. A baby cat
17. A machine that flies

Second Grade Bound © Carson-Dellosa • CD-704635

Circus Sights

Find the answers to the puzzle in the Word Bank.

Across
1. To save from danger
4. The last act
6. A silly person
8. Your mistake
10. To give an order
11. A poster

Down
2. A large weapon
3. A show with clowns and animal acts
5. You dress up in these
7. Great
9. A person who trains animals
11. A trick

Word Bank

cannon	costumes	command	trainer
grand	circus	rescue	clown
fault	stunt	sign	finale

Hidden Mystery

Read the clues. Find the matching words in the Word Bank and write them on the lines. Then find each two-letter mystery word by circling the letters that are the same in each set of matching words. Write each mystery word on a magnifying glass.

1. Something you put on a hot dog _____
2. Outside part of bread _____
3. Dance or sing to . . . _____
4. Someone who might be guilty _____

   The hidden mystery word is _____

1. Words you can sing _____
2. Not weak _____
3. A small rock _____
4. A round fastener _____

   The hidden mystery word is _____

1. A note asking you to a party _____
2. Start _____
3. The meal you eat at night _____
4. A part of a fish _____

   The hidden mystery word is _____

Word Bank			
strong	dinner	fin	stone
invitation	begin	crust	song
button	music	mustard	suspect

We're Just Hopping!

Find and circle the words in the puzzle.
Look → and ↓ .

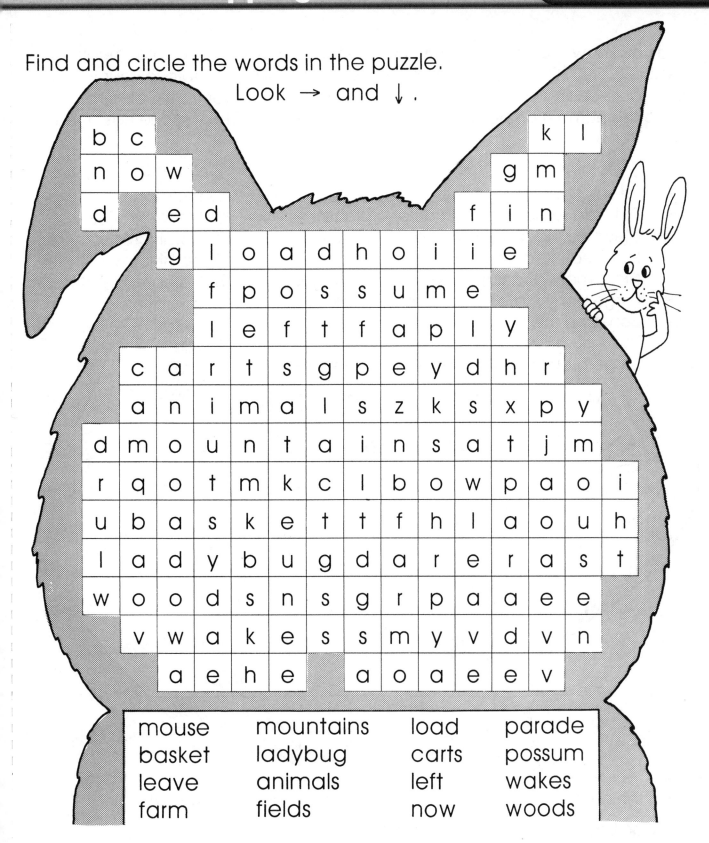

mouse	mountains	load	parade
basket	ladybug	carts	possum
leave	animals	left	wakes
farm	fields	now	woods

Magic Square Mania

Did you know that the word **dinosaur** comes from two Greek words meaning "terrible lizard"? Dinosaurs were not lizards at all! To further improve your dinosaur vocabulary, read Column A. Choose an answer from Column B. Write the number of the answer in the Magic Square. The first one has been done for you.

Column A

A. Person who studies fossils
B. Petrified remains of animals and plants
C. Meat-eating dinosaurs
D. Plant-eating dinosaurs
E. Movement of animals over long distances
F. Large bony plates on dinosaur's neck
G. Bones on the top of a dinosaur's head
H. The Age of Dinosaurs
I. Large groups of animals that live together

Column B

1. skeleton
2. Mesozoic Age
3. carnivores
4. herbivores
5. paleontologist
6. migration
7. herds
8. frills
9. crest
10. fossils

A 5	B	C
D	E	F
G	H	I

Add the numbers across, down and diagonally. What answer do you get? ____

Why do you think this is called a magic square? _____

Body Works

Read the clues. Write the words in the puzzle.

Across:

2. You use these to breathe.
4. You need to do this when you're tired.
5. This breaks down food.
7. This tells your body what to do.
9. A gas you breathe.
10. It pumps blood.

Down:

1. It carries oxygen to your body.
3. Microscopic living things that can make you sick.
6. This helps when you are sick.
8. These support and shape your body.

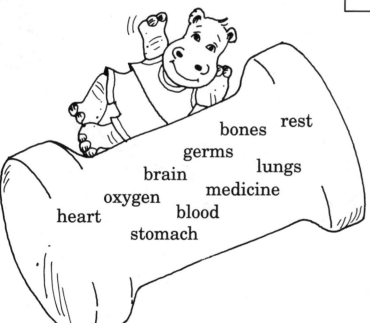

bones   rest
germs
brain   lungs
oxygen   medicine
heart   blood
stomach

Interesting Invertebrates

Invertebrates are animals that have no backbone or inside skeleton. Some have soft bodies protected by shells. Others have soft bodies that are not protected. Some invertebrates are so small that they can only be seen with a microscope.

Below are some examples of invertebrates. Use the clues to name each one.

_ _ _ _ _ _ I P E D E

S _ _ _ _ F _ _ _ _ _

J _ _ _ _ _

F _ _ _ _

E _ _ _ _ W _ _ _ _

S _ _ _ _

D _ _ _ _ _ _ _ _

S _ _ _ _ _

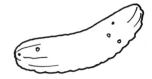

S _ _ _ C _ _ _ _ _ _ _ _

Fine, Feathered Friends

Do the puzzle about birds.
Color only the birds.

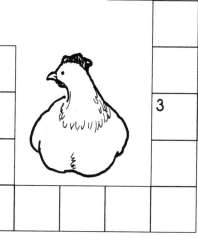

Down

1. _____ keep a bird's body warm and dry.
4. A bird uses its _____ to pick up food.

Across

2. A bird is a _____ -blooded animal.
3. Baby birds are hatched from _____.
5. Birds breathe with their _____.

Word Bank
feathers   bill   lungs   eggs   warm

Name _____

Birds are the only animals that have feathers. All birds have wings, but not all can fly. They all hatch from eggs, have backbones, and are warm-blooded.

The eggs in the nest contain names of different birds. When filling in the puzzle, the last letter of one name becomes the first letter of the next name. Write the names of the birds in the puzzle in the correct order. Start at the outside edge and spiral in toward the center. The first three names are written for you.

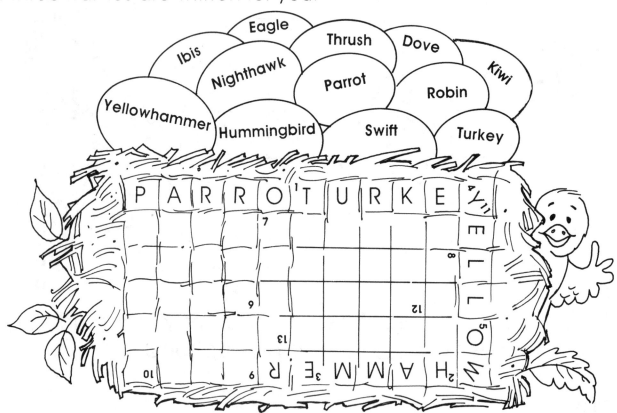

Complete this story. Write the letters from the sections with numbers in the blanks.

A sly and hungry fox quietly crept into the hen house one night. Carefully, he took a basket and began filling it with eggs. As he turned to leave, he tripped on a rake and went tumbling down, eggs and all. The hens awoke, laughed loudly, and said,

"___ ___ ___   ___ ___ ___ ___ ___'   ___ ___   ___ ___ ___!"
  1 2 3   4 5 6 7 8   9 10   11 12 13

A Mixture of Mammals

Mammals live in many different places. They are a special group because they . . .

- can give milk to their babies.
- protect and guide their young.
- are warm-blooded.
- have hair at some time during their lives.
- have a large, well-developed brain.

Below are some silly pictures made from two mammals put together. Write the names of the two real mammals on the lines. The last letter(s) in the name of the first animal is the first letter(s) in the name of the second animal. The first one is done for you.

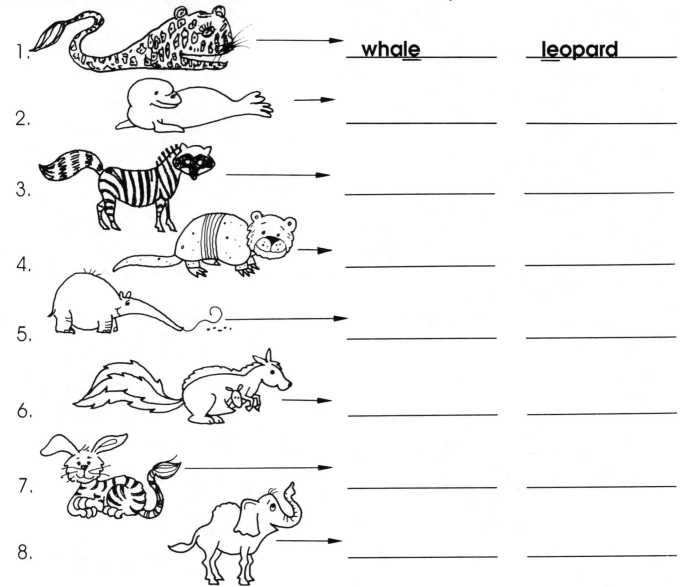

1. <u>whale</u>   <u>leopard</u>

2. _____   _____

3. _____   _____

4. _____   _____

5. _____   _____

6. _____   _____

7. _____   _____

8. _____   _____

Dynamic Dinosaurs

Dinosaurs were reptiles that lived millions of years ago. Some of them were the biggest animals to ever live on land. Some were as small as chickens. Some dinosaurs ate plants, while others were meat-eaters.

Scientists have given names to the dinosaurs that often describe their special bodies, sizes, and habits.

Look at the object(s) placed in the picture with each dinosaur. Use the objects as clues to fill in the blanks and finish each dinosaur's name.

T R I C E R A _____ _____ _____ _____

_____ _____ _____ _____ E O S A U R U S

_____ _____ _____ T R O D O N

_____ _____ _____ A S A U R U S   _____ _____ _____ _____ O S A U R U S

Dial a Dinosaur

Danny loves dinosaurs. In fact, he loves them so much that everyone calls him Dinosaur Danny! Find out what Dinosaur Danny's favorite dinosaur is by decoding the message below. To do this, use the numbers on the telephone and the directional markers.

For example: `3` points to the letter D.

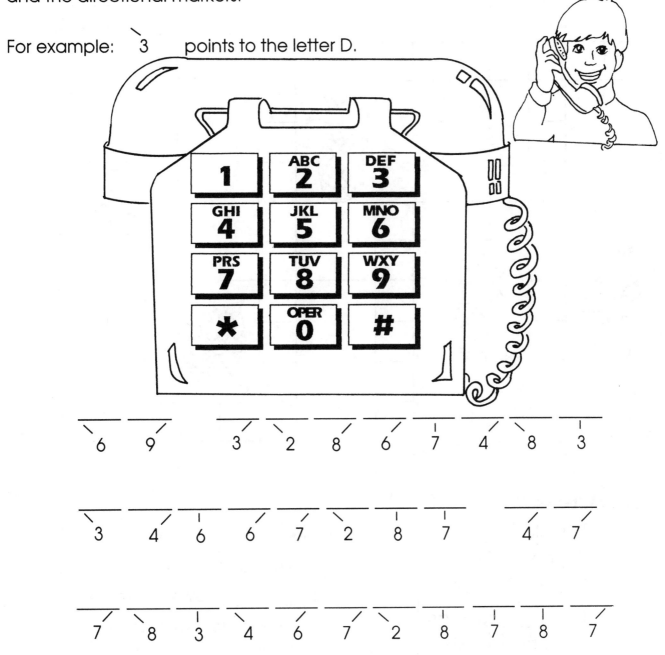

Write your own message and share it with a friend.

Hawaii

Fill in the crossword puzzle. The Word Bank will help you.

Word Bank

Hawaii
mountains
islands
sugar
pineapple
flowers
eight

Across

2. Colorful _____ grow in Hawaii.
4. The 50th state
6. _____ cane grows on the islands.
7. Hawaii has _____ large islands.

Down

1. The islands are _____.
3. _____ grows in Hawaii.
5. Hawaii is made up of many _____.

Follow That Sign!

Look at the road sign symbols below. Each sign is matched to a letter. Use the road sign code to find the names of four vehicles that travel on roads.

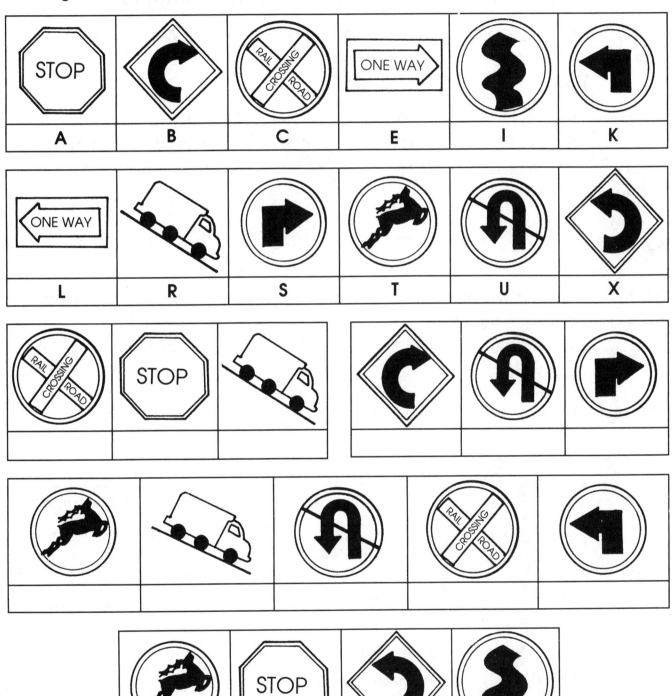

From the Inside Out

Animals whose skeletons have backbones are called **vertebrates**. The backbone, or spine, is made up of bones called **vertebrae**.

Look at the skeletons below. Use the riddle and the Word Bank to write the name of each vertebrate.

1. 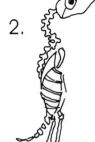 I stand tall and proud. So please don't ask me to eat from the ground.

    I am a _____.

5.  I am thankful to be alive at holidays. People might "gobble me up!"

    I am a _____.

2. I have wings, but I cannot fly. I love to strut around in my "tuxedo."

    I am a _____.

6. 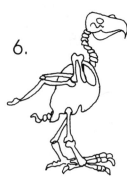 They say I have no hair, and they're right. I represent a great country.

    I am a _____.

3.  I am not a bird, but I can fly. Bruce Wayne used me as a model for his costume.

    I am a _____.

4. My legs and tail are very strong. I even come with a pocket.

    I am a _____.

Word Bank
bald eagle
kangaroo
turkey
penguin
giraffe
bat

Whose House?

Use the pictures of the Native American houses to answer the riddles.

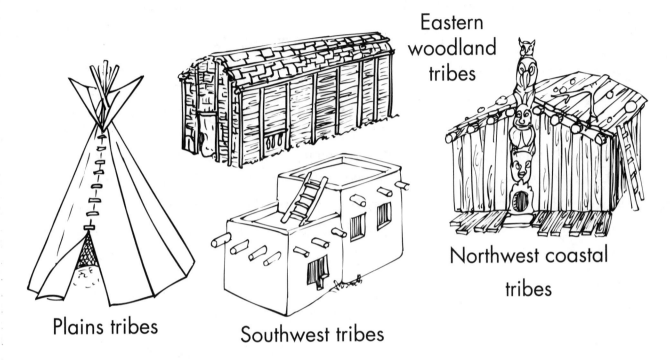

Eastern
woodland
tribes

Plains tribes

Southwest tribes

Northwest coastal
tribes

This house has no beds. Many families live in it. It is made of adobe brick. It has no doors, only windows. Whose house is it? _____	This is called a "plank house." Many families live in it. It is made of large beams and trees. It has a totem pole in front. Whose house is it? _____
This is called a "long house." It has bunk beds. It is made of branches and bark. Fire burns in the center of it. Whose house is it? _____	This house can be set up in 10 minutes. One family lives in it. It is made of poles and animal skins. A fire burns inside. Whose house is it? _____

A Family of Friends

There was a great exhibit at the Museum of American History of figures of Native Americans and Pilgrims sharing the first Thanksgiving feast. When the Pilgrims came to Plymouth, Massachusetts, in 1620, they had a very difficult year. Native Americans helped the Pilgrims hunt and harvest food.

Read each riddle. Use the Word Box to write each food that the Native Americans helped the Pilgrims find or grow.

1. Water doesn't stick –
    It rolls off my back;
    And when it does,
    I loudly say, "Quack, quack!"

    I am _____ .

2. I'm not inside a whale,
    But I'm found in a "wheel."
    You'll also find me
    In a piece of "steel."

    I am _____ .

3. When your roof "leaks,"
    You may want to cry.
    You'll do the same thing
    When I'm near your eye.

    I am _____ .

4. Boil me or pop me
    When I am ripe.
    Cook me in bread
    Or use my cob as a pipe.

    I am _____

5. I like to "honk,"
    And I can fly.
    Ask the lady who rode me,
    Reciting rhymes in the sky.

    I am _____ .

Word Box		
a goose	a leek	a duck
corn	an eel	

Landform Riddles

Use the Word Bank to solve the riddles. Then color the pictures.

Word Bank

| lake | island | plain | river | mountain | peninsula |

I have water on three sides. I am a

_ _ _ _ _ _ _ _ _

I have water all around me. I am an

_ _ _ _ _ _

I am wet and have land all around me. I am a

_ _ _ _

I am long and narrow and flow through the land. I am a

_ _ _ _ _ _ _

I am raised land, larger than a hill. I am a

_ _ _ _ _ _ _ _

I am low and flat. I am a

_ _ _ _ _ _

The Reptile House

There are about 6,000 different kinds of reptiles. They come in all sorts of shapes and colors. Their sizes in length range from 2 inches to almost 30 feet. Reptiles can be found on every continent except Antarctica. Even though reptiles can seem quite different, they all...

- breathe with lungs.
- are cold-blooded.
- have dry, scaly skin.
- have a backbone.

In the Reptile House at the zoo, each animal needs to be placed in the correct area. Read the information about each reptile. Then use the clues and the pictures to write the name of each reptile in its area.

Giant Tortoise can live over 100 years. It can hide under its shell for protection.

Reticulated Python is the longest snake. One was almost 33 feet long.

Saltwater Crocodile is one of the largest reptiles. It can weigh 1,000 lb.

Komodo Dragon is a dragon-like reptile. It is the largest living lizard.

Tuatara is closely related to the extinct dinosaur.

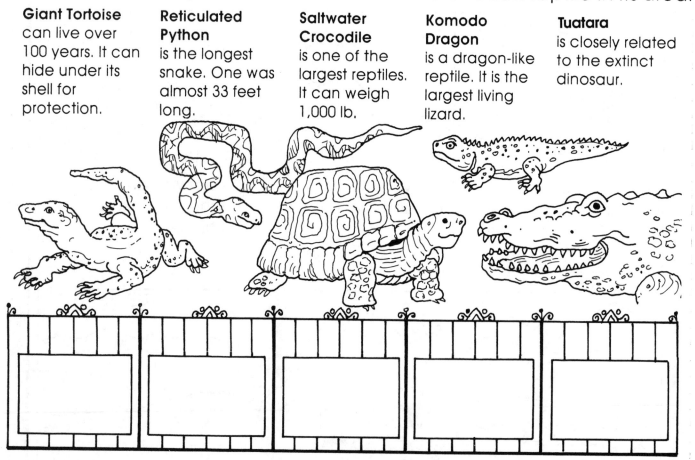

Clues:
- The snake is between the largest lizard and the largest member of the turtle family.
- A relative of the alligator is on the far right side.
- The reptile who carries its "house" is in the middle.

Pottery Patterns

Before beginning a project, an artist who makes pottery must think about how the piece will be used, what type of clay to use, and what color and patterns to use.

This talented artist does something special with all the pottery he makes. Here are some examples of his pottery.

The pottery here is not his. Something is different.

Circle the pottery below that the talented artist might have made.

What is special about his pottery? _____

Dressing the Part

People who act in plays are called **actors** and **actresses**. For each play, costumes are chosen that make the characters in the story seem more realistic.

Below is the inside of a costume closet.

Pretend that you want to act in some silly plays. Look at the titles of each play below. Write the names of the two costumes you would combine to fit the main character of each play.

1. "The Strong, Flying Ape" _____ _____

2. "The Invisible Man on His Horse" _____ _____

3. "The Cat Who Squeaked" _____ _____

4. "Her Royal Highness Barks up the Wrong Tree"

   _____ _____

5. "Flying Animal-like Man Saves Building from Fire" _____

   _____

Everyone is Welcome

Cut out the pictures of the people at the bottom of the page. Read the clues carefully. Paste the people where they belong at the table.

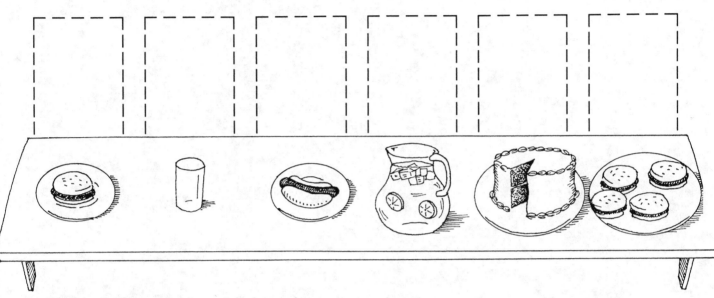

1. Robert already has his hamburger.

2. Kioko will pass the plate of hamburgers to the others at the table.

3. Mike asks Teresa to please pass the pitcher of lemonade so that he may fill his glass.

4. Pablo likes sitting between his friends Kioko and Teresa.

5. Sue likes hot dogs better than hamburgers.

Cut ---

| Pablo | Kioko | Robert | Sue | Mike | Teresa |

Comparing the Seasons

Each of the four seasons (winter, spring, summer, autumn) has certain characteristics. Choose two of the seasons and write their names on the lines above each shape below. Then, complete the other lines with words that describe the season. In the center area, write words that describe both seasons. This is called a **Venn diagram**.

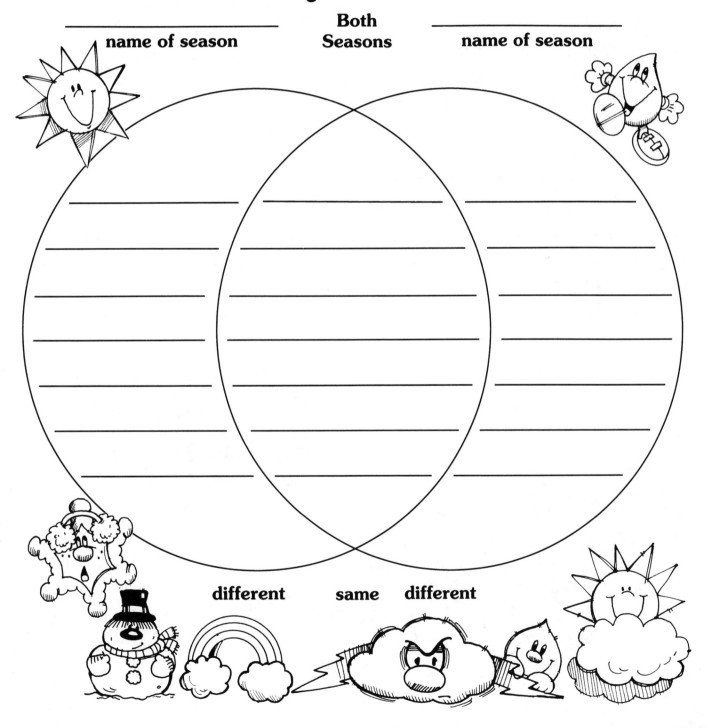

_____
name of season

Both Seasons

_____
name of season

different   same   different

Lazy One Liners

Use your laziest imagination to finish these lazy lines. An example would be, "The lion was so lazy that. . .he made his mate roar for him." Choose three of your best one liners and illustrate them on another paper.

1. The doctor was so lazy that _____

2. The baker was so lazy that _____

3. The teacher was so lazy that _____

4. The fireman was so lazy that _____

5. The dentist was so lazy that _____

6. The truck driver was so lazy that _____

7. The vet was so lazy that _____

8. The plumber was so lazy that _____

9. The house builder was so lazy that _____

10. The principal was so lazy that _____

11. The astronaut was so lazy that _____

12. The football player was so lazy that _____

13. The zookeeper was so lazy that _____

14. The TV repairman was so lazy that _____

15. The traffic cop was so lazy that _____

Name ___________________________

A Story for the People

Look carefully at the picture on the buckskin. Write a story on the lines to tell what is happening in the picture.

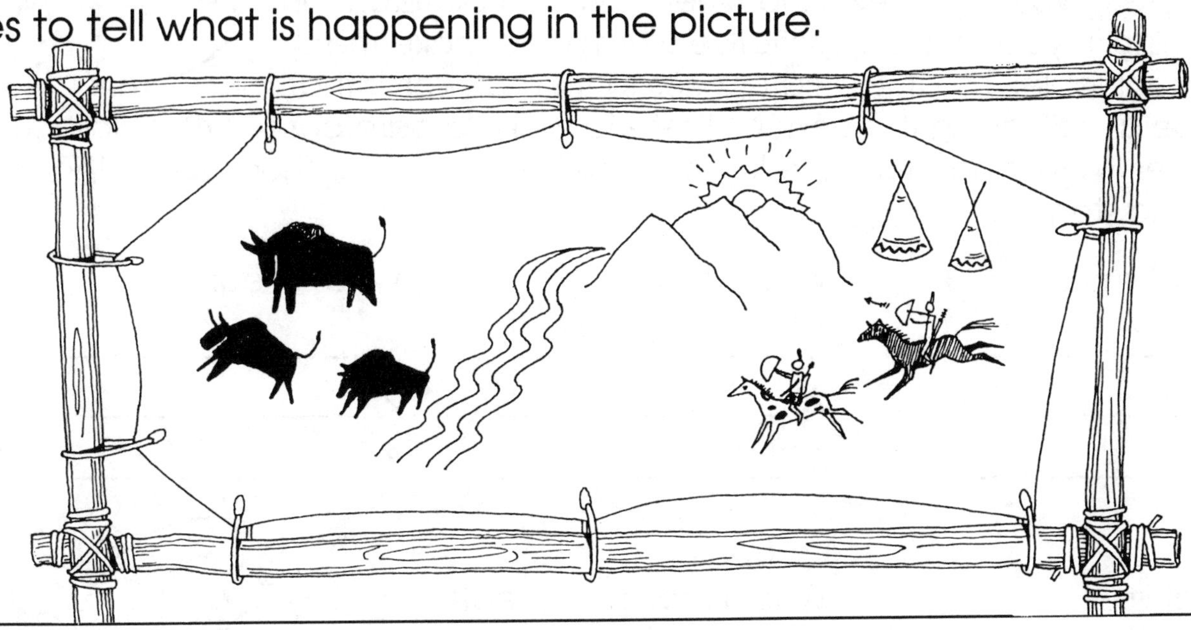

Using Descriptive Language

Stories are always more exciting when you can picture them happening in your mind. Descriptive words help make the story imaginable. Use these categories to think of words that describe a walk along the beach. Pretend you are barefoot walking close to the water. With a partner, write three words in each area. Then, use all the words in a story.

What I smell:

1. _____
2. _____
3. _____

What I taste:

1. _____
2. _____
3. _____

What I hear:

1. _____
2. _____
3. _____

What I see:

1. _____
2. _____
3. _____

What I feel on my feet:

1. _____
2. _____
3. _____

My Walk Along the Beach

_____

_____

_____

_____

_____

_____

_____

_____

Ready to Mail

Read the envelope Tilly addressed to Mr. Bunny.

tilly mole
102 garden road
forest maine 25136

mr bunny
523 sweet potato lane
forest maine 25136

Address the envelope correctly. Be sure to use capital letters, periods and commas where they belong.

_____
_____
_____

_____
_____
_____

Draw and color a stamp on the envelope.

Write, Please

Read the thank you letter Louis wrote to his Uncle McAllister.

october 5 2014

dear uncle mcallister
      thank you for the tadpole   i named him
alphonse   he likes to eat cheeseburgers   this is the
best gift you ever sent me
      thank you again
                  love
                  louis

Write the letter correctly. Be sure to use capital letters, periods and commas where they belong.

_____

_____

_____

_____

_____

_____

_____

_____

_____

_____

Writing Haiku Poetry

Haiku poetry is originally from the country of Japan. It is a very simple form of poetry and does not have to rhyme.

Example	**Poem Pattern**
The polar bear cubs	5 syllables
learn to swim and dive for fish	7 syllables
in the cold, blue sea.	5 syllables

Write your own haiku poem by yourself or with a partner. Give it a title and illustrate it.

_____
Title

_____

- -

_____

- -

_____

- -

_____

By a Beary Special Poet _____
Name

Read the following skills aloud. Ask your child to place a check mark in each box once he or she has mastered the second grade skill.

- ❑ ABC Order
- ❑ Consonants
- ❑ Vowels
- ❑ Syllables
- ❑ Compound Words
- ❑ Synonyms and Antonyms
- ❑ Similes
- ❑ Nouns, Verbs, and Adjectives
- ❑ Sentences
- ❑ Capitalization and Punctuation
- ❑ Comparative Adjectives

- ❑ Drawing Conclusions
- ❑ Fact and Opinion
- ❑ Following Directions
- ❑ Sequencing
- ❑ Classifying
- ❑ Cause and Effect
- ❑ Comprehension
- ❑ Main Idea
- ❑ Critical Thinking
- ❑ Writing

Now, try these fun learning activities!

Try these hands-on activities for enhancing your child's learning and development. Be sure to encourage speaking, listening, touching, and active movement.

- Play a silly game with your child. Take turns naming three things, such as **bread**, **butter**, and **pencil**. Ask your child to name which one does not belong and why.
- Discuss and list both good and bad manners. Teach appropriate manners at the dinner table, at a movie theater, and at a restaurant through role-playing.
- Have your child paint a rainbow. When the paint dries, ask your child to dictate a sentence about each color of the rainbow. Write each sentence on the arc of its color.

Math

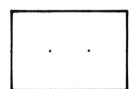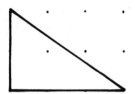

Be positive and encouraging as your child encounters new academic skills. Don't worry if your child doesn't understand everything immediately. Instead, pay attention to what your child already knows well and then help him or her tackle new challenges. With enough practice, your child will begin to understand and master the concepts. That's why it's good to begin preparing for second grade now, so that he or she has every possible advantage!

As you continue to work through this book, explain the activities in terms your child understands, and encourage him or her to talk about the pictures and activities. These conversations will both strengthen your child's confidence and build important language skills.

This Math section will cover important skills your child needs to know, including:

- Counting
- Skip Counting
- Addition
- Subtraction
- Regrouping
- Problem Solving
- Estimation
- Ordinal Numbers
- Comparing Numbers

- Time
- Money
- Measurement
- Volume
- Patterns
- Geometry
- Fractions
- Graphing
- Multiplication

Just Napping

Count. Write the correct number of cats in the box on each cat bed.

Unpacking the Teddy Bears

Cut out the bears at the bottom of the page. Paste them where they belong in numbered order.

Cut ✂ -

Plump Piglets

Pigs like to eat corn. These little pigs just ate lunch.

Read the clues to find out how many ears of corn each pig ate. Write the number on the line below each pig.

Who ate the most and was really piggy? _____

Who ate the least? _____

Name _____

Finish counting.

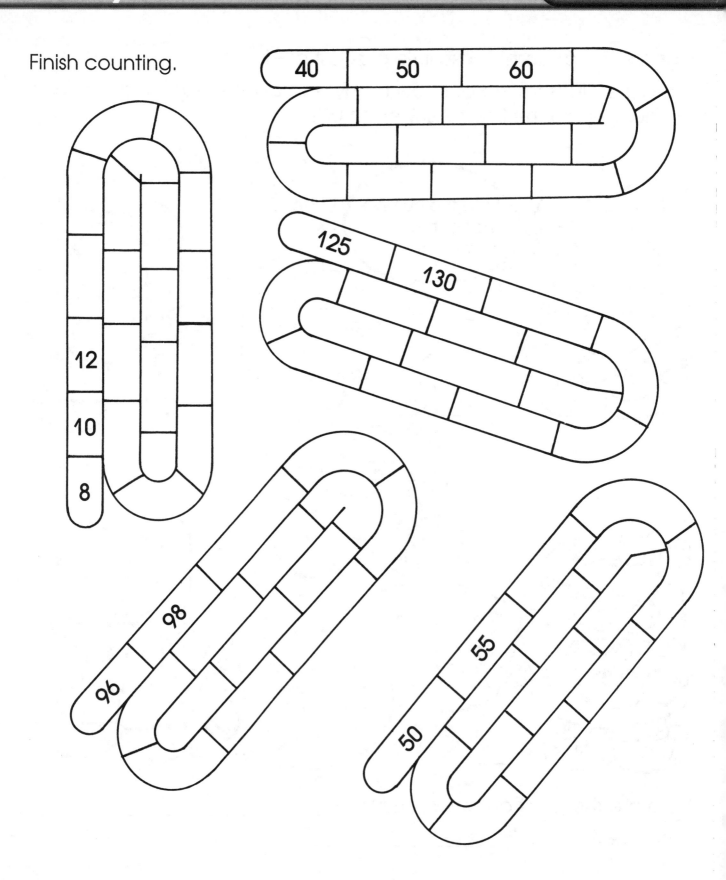

40 50 60

125

130

12

10

8

98

96

55

50

Name _____

Critter Count

Number of 's found.    = 5

 = 20

   = ____

 = ____

Number of 's found.    = 10

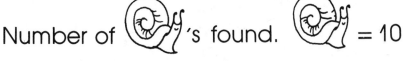 = ____

        = ____

= ____

Number of 's found. = 2

= ____

 = ____

= ____

Air Bear Addition

Help Buddy off the ground. Solve the problems. Then color the clouds with sums of 9 to find the right path.

5
+5

7
+4

3
+7

4
+4

6
+3

7
+1

6
+4

2
+7

2
+5

10
+1

5
+4

6
+5

3
+4

3
+2

2
+5

0
+9

4
+5

9
+0

2
+6

8
+2

3
+6

Math-Minded Mermaids

Each mermaid sits upon her own special rock.

Look at the number on each shell. Then look → and ↓ in the number boxes. Circle each pair of numbers that can be added together to equal the number in the shell the mermaid is holding.

Domino Math

Write the number that tells how many dots are on the greater side of each domino. Then, "count on" to find the sum of both sides.

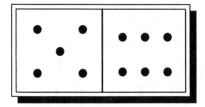

_____

sum _____

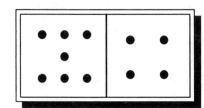

_____

sum _____

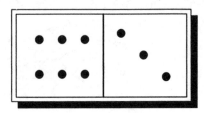

_____

sum _____

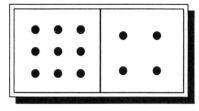

_____

sum _____

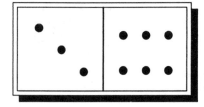

_____

sum _____

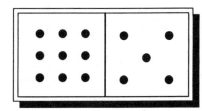

_____

sum _____

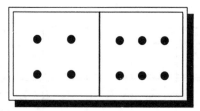

_____

sum _____

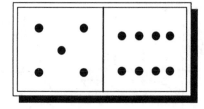

_____

sum _____

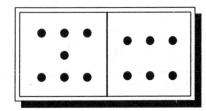

_____

sum _____

Ride the Rapids

Write each problem on the life jacket with the correct answer.

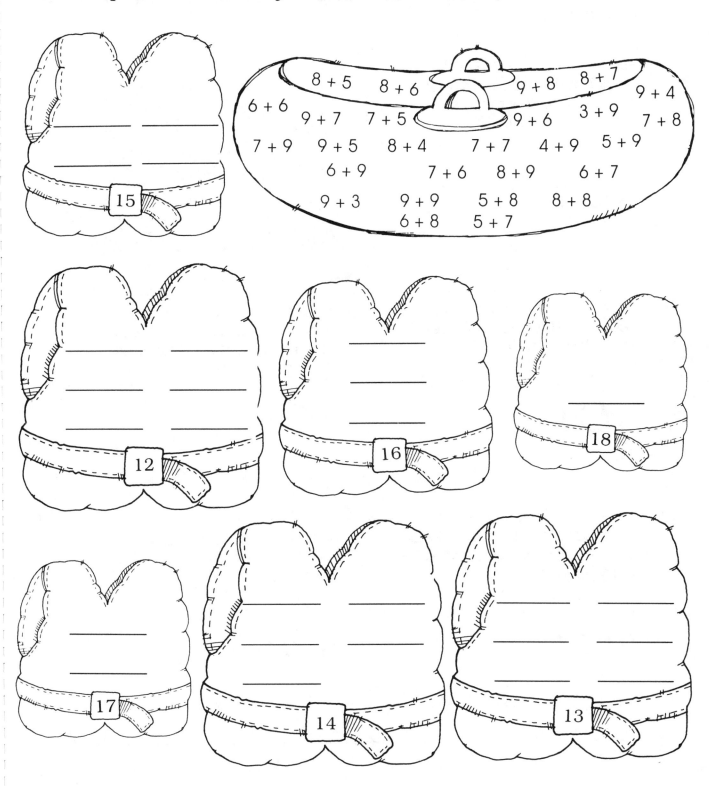

Name _____

The key words **in all** tell you to add. Circle the key words **in all** and solve the problems.

1. Jack has 4 white shirts and 2 yellow shirts. How many shirts does Jack have in all?

$$4 \oplus 2 = \underline{\hspace{1cm}}$$

2. Joan has 4 pink blouses and 6 red ones. How many blouses does Joan have in all?

$$4 \bigcirc 6 = \underline{\hspace{1cm}}$$

3. Mack has 3 pairs of summer pants and 8 pairs of winter pants. How many pairs of pants does Mack have in all?

$$3 \bigcirc 8 = \underline{\hspace{1cm}}$$

4. Betsy has 2 black skirts and 7 blue skirts. In all, how many skirts does Betsy have?

$$2 \bigcirc 7 = \underline{\hspace{1cm}}$$

5. Willis has 5 knit hats and 5 cloth hats. How many hats does Willis have in all?

$$5 \bigcirc 5 = \underline{\hspace{1cm}}$$

Additional Story Problems

Circle the addition key words **in all** and solve the problems.

1. On the block where Cindy lives there are 7 brick houses and 5 stone houses. How many houses are there in all?

$$7 + 5 = \underline{\hspace{1.5cm}}$$

2. One block from Cindy's house there are 7 white houses and 4 gray houses. How many houses are there in all?

3. Near Cindy's house there are 3 grocery stores and 5 discount stores. How many stores are there in all?

4. Children live in 8 of the two-story houses, and children live in 2 of the one-story houses. How many houses in all have children living in them?

5. In Cindy's neighborhood 4 students are in high school and 9 are in elementary school. In all, how many children are in school?

Problems in the Park

Circle the addition key words **in all** and solve the problems.

1. At the park there are 3 baseball games and 6 basketball games being played. How many games are being played in all?

2. In the park 9 mothers are pushing their babies in strollers, and 8 are carrying their babies in baskets. How many mothers in all have their babies with them in the park?

3. On one team there are 6 boys and 3 girls. How many team members are there in all?

4. At one time there were 8 men and 4 boys pitching horseshoes. In all, how many people were pitching horseshoes?

5. While playing basketball, 4 of the players were wearing gym shoes and 6 were not. How many basketball players were there in all?

Solving Stories

Write a number sentence to solve each problem.

1. Brad ate five slices of pizza. Todd ate three. How many slices of pizza did both boys eat?

2. Sam scored four points for the team. Dave scored eight points. How many points did Sam and Dave score?

3. Missy bought six dresses. Dot bought two. How many dresses did they buy in all?

4. Three bears are having a picnic. Two more bears join the fun. How many bears are having a picnic now?

5. Matt has a barn. In the barn are four horses, three cows and five pigs. How many animals are in the barn?

Training with Facts

Use the numbers on each train to write the fact families.

___ + ___ = ___

___ + ___ = ___

___ − ___ = ___

___ − ___ = ___

___ + ___ = ___

___ + ___ = ___

___ − ___ = ___

___ − ___ = ___

___ + ___ = ___

___ + ___ = ___

___ − ___ = ___

___ − ___ = ___

___ + ___ = ___

___ + ___ = ___

___ − ___ = ___

___ − ___ = ___

Adding Strategies

When adding three numbers, add two numbers first, then add the third to that sum. To decide which two numbers to add first, try one of these strategies.

| Look for doubles. |

```
  8                4 ⟩ 8          2
  3 ⟩ 6            4              9 ⟩ 4
+ 3               + 5            + 2
─────             ─────         ─────
 14                13             13
```

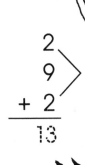

| Look for a ten. |

```
  7 ⟩ 10           8              1
  3                4 ⟩ 10         5 ⟩ 10
+ 4               + 6            + 9
─────             ─────         ─────
 14                18             15
```

Try these. Look for a 10 or doubles.

```
    5          2          7          3          6
    5          6          1          7          2
  + 4        + 8        + 7        + 4        + 6
  ─────      ─────      ─────      ─────      ─────


    7          7          6          5
    6          8          7          5
  + 6        + 3        + 4        + 3
  ─────      ─────      ─────      ─────
```

Sum Ice Cream

Add. If the sum is 11 or more, color the cone **brown**. If the sum is less than 11, color the cone **yellow**.

Add. Show the detective the correct path. Color the path with sums of 13.

6 + 4 + 3

6 + 5 + 5

$\begin{array}{r} 9 \\ 1 \\ + 5 \\ \hline \end{array}$

$\begin{array}{r} 7 \\ 3 \\ + 3 \\ \hline \end{array}$

$\begin{array}{r} 8 \\ 3 \\ + 1 \\ \hline \end{array}$

8 + 4 + 2

4 + 4 + 5

$\begin{array}{r} 5 \\ 6 \\ + 4 \\ \hline \end{array}$

$\begin{array}{r} 9 \\ 8 \\ + 1 \\ \hline \end{array}$

$\begin{array}{r} 5 \\ 3 \\ + 5 \\ \hline \end{array}$

2 + 9 + 2

$\begin{array}{r} 4 \\ 6 \\ + 4 \\ \hline \end{array}$

2 + 8 + 7

Something's Missing

In the forest, 13 animals have a picnic. Skunk brings 8 sandwiches. How many sandwiches should Raccoon bring so that each animal can have one?

$$8 + \underline{\ ?\ } = 13$$

What number added to 8 equals 13?

To find the missing addend, find the difference of 13 and 8. That is, subtract the given addend (8) from the sum (13).

$$13 - 8 = \underline{\ 5\ }$$

Since 13 − 8 = 5, then 8 + $\underline{\ 5\ }$ = 13.

Raccoon should bring $\underline{\ 5\ }$ sandwiches.

Try these. Find the missing addends.

$\underline{\quad} + 6 = 15$ $\qquad\qquad$ $\underline{\quad} + 7 = 13$

$9 + \underline{\quad} = 14$ $\qquad\qquad$ $8 + \underline{\quad} = 14$

$\underline{\quad} + 8 = 16$ $\qquad\qquad$ $9 + \underline{\quad} = 18$

Food Fun

The table below tells what each animal brought to the picnic.
Fill in the missing numbers.

Animal	Vegetables	Fruits	Total
Skunk	8	6	14
Raccoon	9		17
Squirrel		8	15
Rabbit	6		13
Owl	7		16
Deer		9	18

Write the name of the animal that answers each question.

1. Who brought the same number of vegetables as fruits?

   _____

2. Who brought two more fruits than vegetables? _____

3. Who brought two more vegetables than fruits? _____

4. Which two animals brought one more fruit than vegetables?

   _____ and _____

5. Which two animals brought the most vegetables?

   _____ and _____

6. Which two animals brought the most fruit? _____ and

   _____

7. Which animal brought the least vegetables? _____

8. Which animal brought the least fruit? _____

9. Who brought more fruit, Skunk and Squirrel, or Raccoon and

   Rabbit? _____

Circus Fun

Add. Remember to add the ones first.

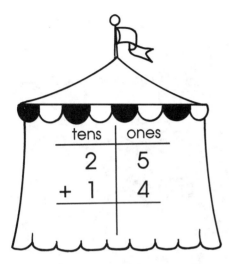

tens	ones
2	5
+ 1	4

tens	ones
5	3
+ 3	2

tens	ones
7	1
+ 2	8

tens	ones
4	4
+ 3	2

tens	ones
5	1
+ 3	7

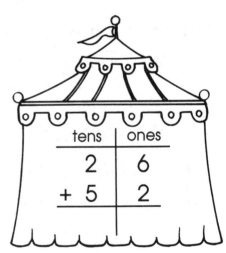

tens	ones
2	6
+ 5	2

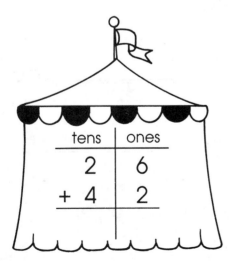

tens	ones
2	6
+ 4	2

tens	ones
3	7
+ 5	1

tens	ones
1	9
+ 3	0

Anchors Away

Add. Use the code to find the answer to this riddle:

What did the pirate have to do before every trip out to sea?

48	36	58	96	69	75	89	29
O	H	G	B	T	E	N	A

	42 + 16	34 + 41	60 + 9
	58		
	(G)		

	17 + 31	55 + 34

26 + 43	14 + 22	52 + 23

83 + 13	24 + 24	5 + 24	52 + 17

Digital Addition

Add ones first.
4 + 2 = 6

tens	ones
2	4
+3	2
	6

Then, add tens.
2 + 3 = 5

tens	ones
2	4
+3	2
5	6

tens	ones
1	7
+2	1

tens	ones
3	4
+5	2

tens	ones
	5
+6	2

tens	ones
	6
+5	2

tens	ones
2	0
+4	0

tens	ones
5	1
+	8

tens	ones
7	2
+1	7

tens	ones
4	7
+2	1

tens	ones
2	5
+6	2

tens	ones
4	2
+2	4

tens	ones
8	3
+1	4

tens	ones
3	2
+2	5

tens	ones
4	4
+3	1

tens	ones
	8
+3	1

tens	ones
6	2
+1	7

tens	ones
8	2
+	7

Nutty Addition

Sam Squirrel and his friend Wendy were gathering acorns. When they got 10 acorns, they put them in a bucket. The picture shows how many acorns Sam and Wendy each gathered. Write the number that tells how many.

tens	ones

_____

tens	ones

_____

How many acorns did Sam and Wendy gather in all? To find out:

1. | Put numbers on tens and ones table. |

tens	ones
3	6
+ 2	7

2. | Add ones first. |

tens	ones
1	
3	6
+ 2	7
	3

Ring 10.
Regroup 13 ones as 1 ten 3 ones.

3. | Add tens. |

tens	ones
1	
3	6
+ 2	7
6	3

Sam and Wendy gathered __63__ in all.

Try this. Add. Regroup as needed.

tens	ones
3	8
+ 4	6

tens	ones
5	4
+ 2	7

tens	ones
4	9
+ 1	3

tens	ones
2	6
+ 1	7

Keep on Truckin'

Write each sum. Connect the sums of 83 to make a road for the truck.

17 + 66	58 + 25	42 + 19	38 + 25

26 + 57	17 + 75	48 + 26	28 + 38	65 + 29

58 + 37	64 + 19	48 + 35	65 + 16	37 + 39

39 + 59	59 + 27	55 + 28	39 + 44

Just Like Magic

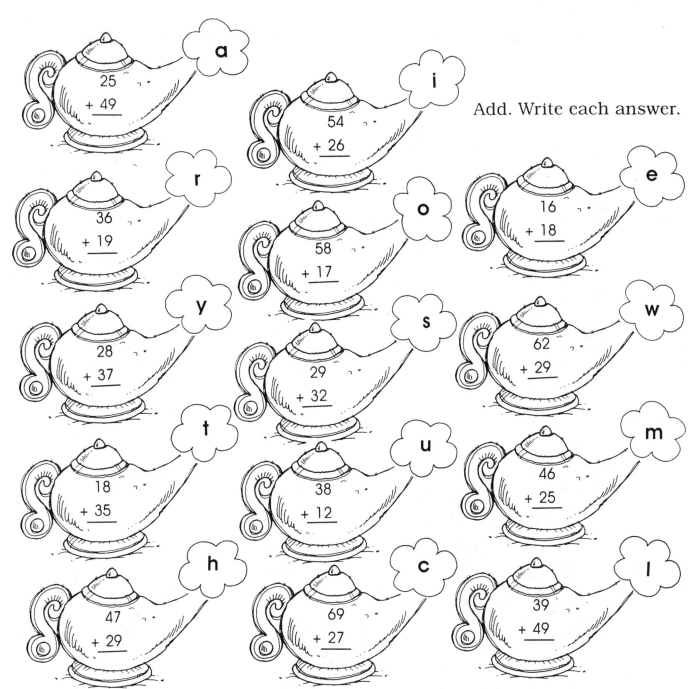

Add. Write each answer.

a
25
+ 49

i
54
+ 26

r
36
+ 19

o
58
+ 17

e
16
+ 18

y
28
+ 37

s
29
+ 32

w
62
+ 29

t
18
+ 35

u
38
+ 12

m
46
+ 25

h
47
+ 29

c
69
+ 27

l
39
+ 49

Use the answers and the letter on each lamp to solve the code.

71 74 65   74 88 88   65 75 50 55

91 80 61 76 34 61   96 75 71 34   53 55 50 34 !

Squirrelly Fun

Add. Regroup as needed. Match the squirrels to their trees.

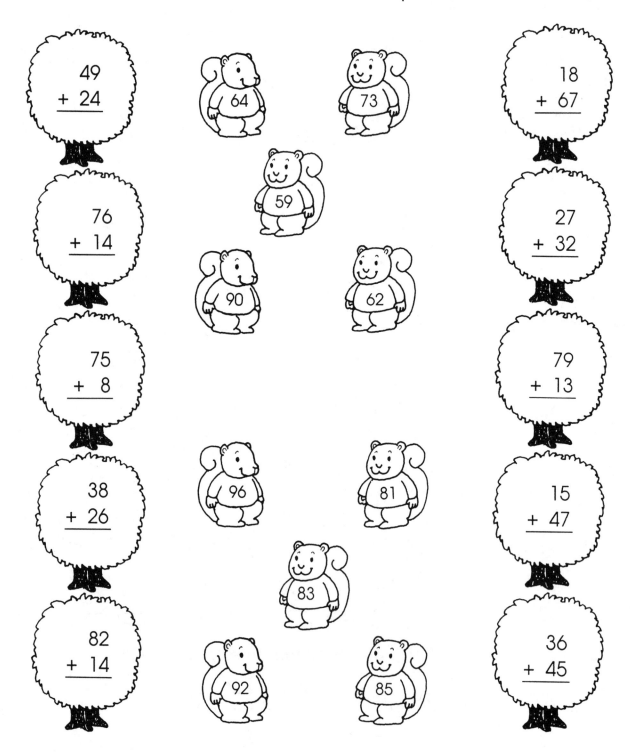

Daisy Subtraction

Subtract.
Use code to color.

2—green	**7**—orange	**10**—pink
3—blue	**8**—red	**11**—red
4—yellow	**9**—purple	**12**—purple

Pick a Picnic

Subtract. Write each answer. Then draw a line to show where three answers are the same in a row.

12 – 9 =	11 – 2 =	9 – 8 =
8 – 6 =	7 – 4 =	7 – 5 =
7 – 3 =	10 – 1 =	11 – 8 =

10 – 7 =	12 – 3 =	11 – 2 =
12 – 7 =	9 – 0 =	8 – 5 =
11 – 4 =	9 – 2 =	12 – 5 =

10 – 4 =	8 – 3 =	8 – 4 =
12 – 4 =	12 – 8 =	8 – 2 =
11 – 7 =	10 – 3 =	11 – 3 =

9 – 7 =	11 – 9 =	10 – 2 =
11 – 5 =	9 – 3 =	12 – 6 =
8 – 1 =	12 – 7 =	9 – 5 =

7 – 7 =	11 – 6 =	9 – 1 =
10 – 3 =	9 – 4 =	10 – 0 =
8 – 8 =	10 – 5 =	12 – 4 =

Connect the Facts

Subtract. Write the answer.

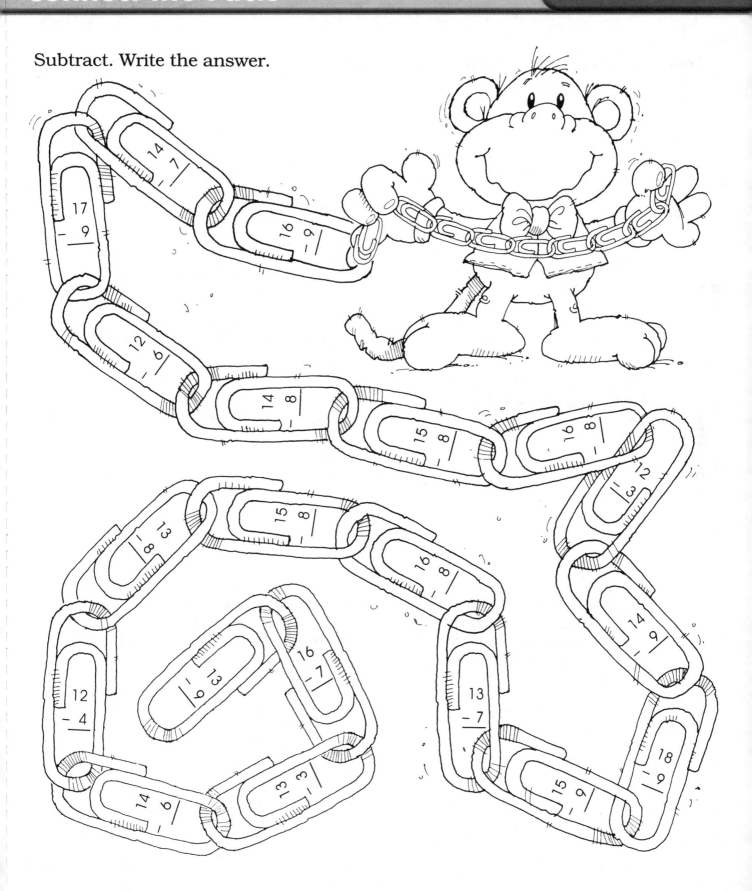

The chain links contain the following subtraction problems:

14 − 7

17 − 9

16 − 9

12 − 6

14 − 8

15 − 8

16 − 8

12 − 3

13 − 8

15 − 8

16 − 8

14 − 9

12 − 4

13 − 9

16 − 7

13 − 7

14 − 9

13 − 3

15 − 9

18 − 9

How Many Animals Are Left?

The key word **left** tells you to subtract. Circle the key word **left** and solve the problems.

1. Bill had 10 kittens, but 4 of them ran away. How many kittens does he have left?

$$10 - 4 = \underline{\hspace{1cm}}$$

2. There were 12 rabbits eating clover. Dogs chased 3 of them away. How many rabbits were left?

3. Bill saw 11 birds eating from the bird feeders in his back yard. A cat scared 7 of them away. How many birds were left at the feeders?

4. There were 14 frogs on the bank of the pond. Then 9 of them hopped into the water. How many frogs were left on the bank?

5. Bill counted 15 robins in his yard. Then 8 of the robins flew away. How many robins were left in the yard?

Maggy at School

Circle the subtraction key word **left** and solve the problems.

1. In Maggy's classroom there are 12 girls. One day 4 of the girls went home with the flu. How many girls were left in school that day?

2. Maggy is in 10 different clubs. This week 5 of them will not meet. How many of Maggy's clubs are left to meet this week?

3. Maggy had 16 crayons. She broke 9 of them. How many crayons does Maggy have left?

4. There are 13 boys in Maggy's classroom. One morning 8 of the boys went to the gym. How many were left in the classroom?

5. One day 4 of the 13 boys were called in from the playground. How many of the boys were left on the playground?

Fishy School

Name _____

Write the numbers and subtract.

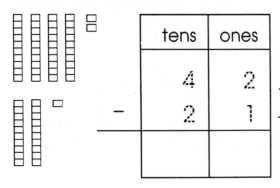

tens	ones
4	2
− 2	1

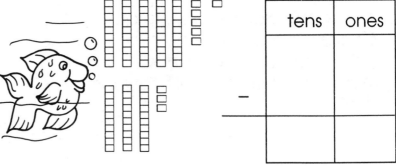

tens	ones
−	

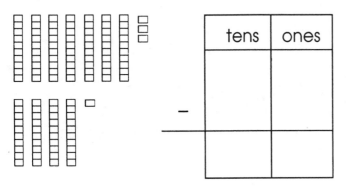

tens	ones
−	

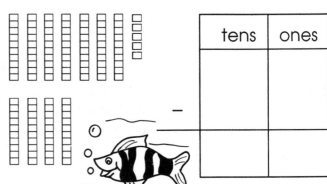

tens	ones
−	

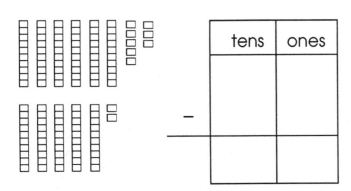

tens	ones
−	

tens	ones
−	

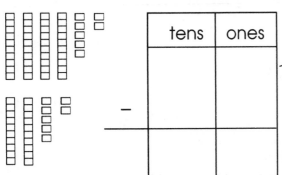

tens	ones
−	

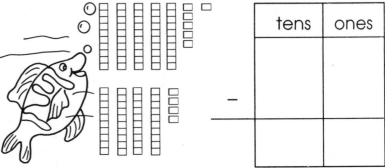

tens	ones
−	

Second Grade Bound © Carson-Dellosa • CD-704635

Name _____

There are 46 cookies.
Bill eats 22 cookies.
How many are left?

$$\begin{array}{r} 46 \\ -\ 22 \\ \hline \end{array}$$

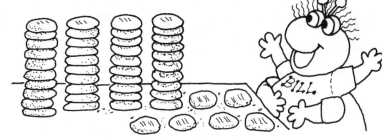

1. | Put numbers on tens and ones table.

tens	ones
4	6
− 2	2

2. | Subtract ones.

tens	ones
4	6
− 2	2
	4

3. | Subtract tens.

tens	ones
4	6
− 2	2
2	4

There are __24__ cookies left.

Try these. Subtract the ones first. Then subtract the tens.

tens	ones
7	8
− 2	5

tens	ones
5	9
− 3	6

tens	ones
8	3
− 6	1

tens	ones
6	7
− 4	3

Rewrite in column form. Subtract ones, then tens.

97 − 14 = ____

tens	ones
−	

54 − 30 = ____

tens	ones
−	

Prehistoric Problems

Subtract. Use color code. **25**—blue, **31**—yellow,
57—green, **14**—orange, **21**—brown, **11**—red

$$47 - 22$$

$$52 - 21$$

$$62 - 31$$

$$25 - 11$$

$$77 - 20$$

$$51 - 40$$

$$55 - 34$$

$$69 - 12$$

$$98 - 41$$

Second Grade Bound © Carson-Dellosa • CD-704635

Cookie Craze!

Subtract. Circle the difference. Color the cookies with differences greater than 30.

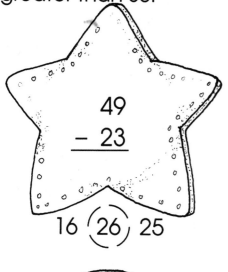

49
− 23

16 (26) 25

67
− 41

26   15   62

58
− 37

81   11   21

75
− 50

20   25   35

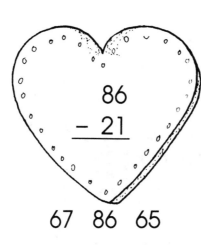

86
− 21

67   86   65

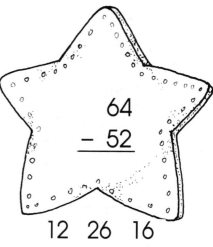

64
− 52

12   26   16

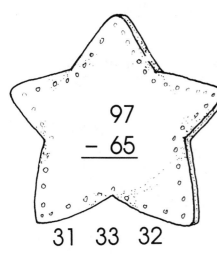

97
− 65

31   33   32

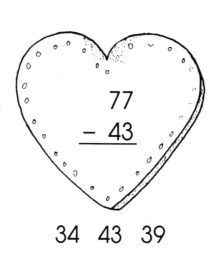

77
− 43

34   43   39

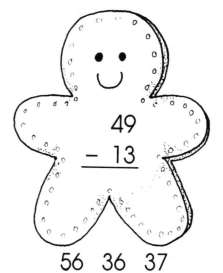

49
− 13

56   36   37

Ellen found 32 shells on the beach. She gave 15 shells to Cindy. How many shells does Ellen have now? To find out:

1. | Put numbers on tens and ones table. |

tens	ones
3	2
− 1	5

2. | Subtract ones. Ask: Do I need to regroup? |

tens	ones
2	12
3̸	2̸
− 1	5
	7

regroup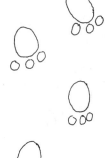

32 = 2 tens and 12 ones

3. | Subtract tens. |

tens	ones
2	12
3̸	2̸
− 1	5
1	7

Ellen has __17__ shells now.

Try this. Subtract. Regroup as needed.

tens	ones
4	1
− 1	7

tens	ones
7	5
− 3	8

tens	ones
5	0
− 2	6

tens	ones
3	6
− 1	9

Name _____

Hatta Boy!

Subtract. Regroup as needed. Write your answers on the hats.

66 – 49

43 – 25

34 – 16

42 – 29

52 – 17

72 – 34

46 – 28

67 – 28

Subtract. Regroup as needed. Color the spaces with differences of:

10-19	red	**30-39**	green
50-59	brown	**20-29**	blue
40-49	yellow	**60-69**	orange

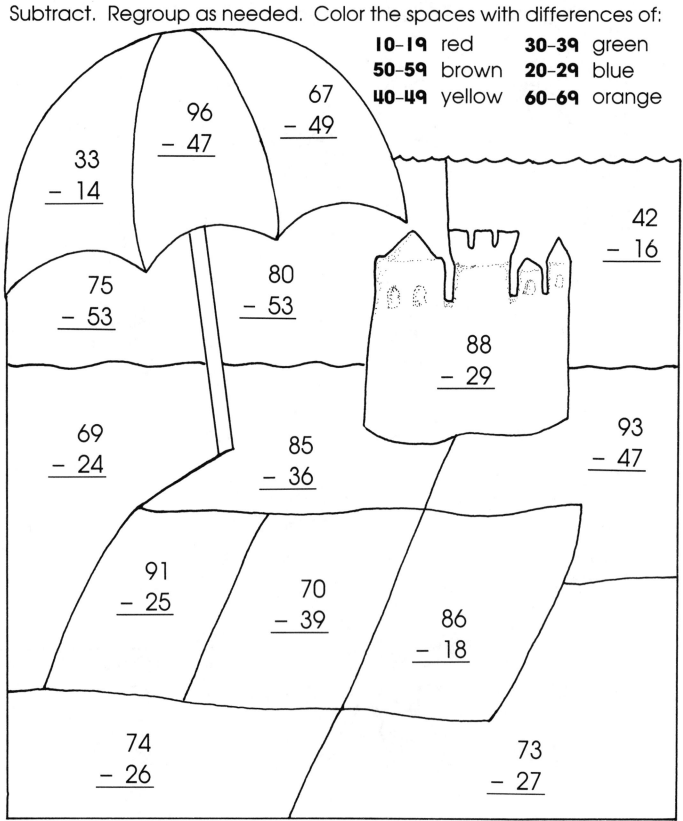

$$33 - 14$$

$$96 - 47$$

$$67 - 49$$

$$42 - 16$$

$$75 - 53$$

$$80 - 53$$

$$88 - 29$$

$$69 - 24$$

$$85 - 36$$

$$93 - 47$$

$$91 - 25$$

$$70 - 39$$

$$86 - 18$$

$$74 - 26$$

$$73 - 27$$

Second Grade Bound © Carson-Dellosa • CD-704635

How's Your Pitch?

Subtract. Write each answer.

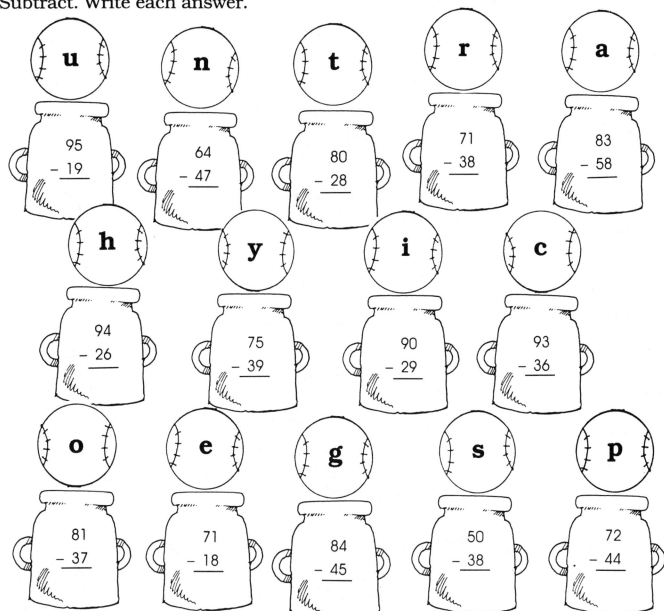

Use the answers and the letters on the baseballs to solve the code.

___ ___ ___ ___   ___ ___ ___ ___ ___   ___ ___
36 44 76 33   28 61 52 57 68   61 12

___ ___ ___ ___ ___   ___ ___   ___ ___ ___ ___ ___ ___ !
33 61 39 68 52   44 17   52 25 33 39 53 52

Match the drivers to their cars.

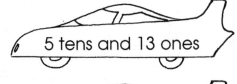
5 tens and 13 ones

84

4 tens and 18 ones

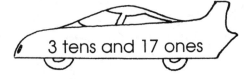
3 tens and 17 ones

16

58

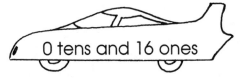
0 tens and 16 ones

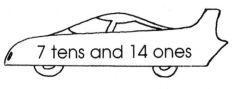
7 tens and 14 ones

63

1 ten and 10 ones

47

Regroup. Write how many tens and ones.

_____ tens and _____ ones

_____ tens and _____ ones

_____ tens and _____ ones

40

35

21

A Hidden Message

Add or subtract. Use the code to find out your new motto!

Code:

9	18	6	15	13	12	16	11	8	7	14	17
H	Y	D	E	V	T	S	O	A	M	N	I

9
+ 8

16	14	8	6
- 7	- 6	+ 5	+ 9

14	9
- 7	+ 9

17	15	9	13	8
- 8	- 7	+ 5	- 7	+ 8

4	6
+ 7	+ 8

12	17	6	15
- 5	- 9	+ 6	- 6

Add or subtract. Match the related facts.

5 + 9 = _14_ •   • 6 + 9 = ___

8 + 7 = ___ •   • 14 − 9 = _5_

15 − 9 = ___ •   • 15 − 7 = ___

17 − 8 = ___ •   • 14 − 7 = ___

7 + 7 = ___ •   • 9 + 8 = ___

Add or subtract. Color spaces with answers greater than 12 **brown**.
Color the rest **green**.

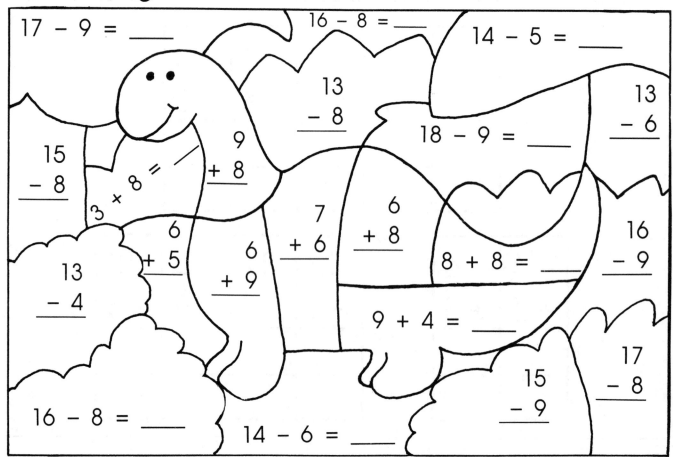

17 − 9 = ___

16 − 8 = ___

14 − 5 = ___

13 − 8

13 − 6

15 − 8

3 + 8 =

9 + 8

18 − 9 = ___

6 + 5

7 + 6

6 + 8

16 − 9

13 − 4

6 + 9

8 + 8 = ___

9 + 4 = ___

16 − 8 = ___

14 − 6 = ___

15 − 9

17 − 8

Add or Subtract?

The key words **in all** tell you to add. The key word **left** tells you to subtract. Circle the key words and solve the problems.

1. The pet store has 3 large dogs and 5 small dogs. How many dogs are there in all?

   3 ⊕ 5 = _____

2. The pet store had 9 parrots and then sold 4 of them. How many parrots does the pet store have left?

   9 ◯ 4 = _____

3. The pet store gave Linda's class 2 adult gerbils and 9 young ones. How many gerbils did Linda's class get in all?

   2 ◯ 9 = _____

4. At the pet store 3 of the 8 myna birds were sold. How many myna birds are left in the pet store?

   8 ◯ 3 = _____

5. The monkey at the pet store has 5 rubber toys and 4 wooden toys. How many toys does it have in all?

   5 ◯ 4 = _____

To find out if the answer to a subtraction problem is correct, add the answer to the number taken away. If the sum is the same as the first number in the subtraction problem, then the answer is correct.

Example 1

$$
\begin{array}{r} 3\ 13 \\ \cancel{43} \\ -\ 27 \\ \hline 16 \end{array}
\longrightarrow
\begin{array}{r} 1 \\ 16 \\ +\ 27 \\ \hline 43 \end{array}
$$

Since the sum is the same as the first number in the subtraction problem, the answer to the subtraction problem must be correct.

Example 2

$$
\begin{array}{r} 6\ 11 \\ \cancel{71} \\ -\ 28 \\ \hline 43 \end{array}
\longrightarrow
\begin{array}{r} 1 \\ 43 \\ +\ 28 \\ \hline 71 \end{array}
$$

Check the subtraction by adding.

$$
\begin{array}{r} 52 \\ -\ 37 \\ \hline 25 \end{array}
\longrightarrow \quad + \ \underline{\quad}
$$

Is the subtraction problem correct? _____
How do you know?

Subtract. Then add to check.

$$
\begin{array}{r} 52 \\ -\ 37 \\ \hline \end{array}
\longrightarrow \quad + \ \underline{\quad}
\qquad
\begin{array}{r} 80 \\ -\ 26 \\ \hline \end{array}
\longrightarrow \quad + \ \underline{\quad}
\qquad
\begin{array}{r} 64 \\ -\ 48 \\ \hline \end{array}
\longrightarrow \quad + \ \underline{\quad}
$$

Playing in the Park

Circle **Add** or **Subtract**. Then, write a number sentence to solve each problem. Think and check to see if your answer makes sense.

1. There are 6 swings. Four children are swinging. How many swings are empty?

   Add   Subtract

____ swings

2. The slide has 8 steps. Craig climbed 3 steps. How many more steps must he climb?

   Add   Subtract

____ steps

3. Ellen went across the monkey bars 5 times. So did Brooke. How many times did both girls go across?

   Add   Subtract

____ times

4. Three girls sat on one park bench. Three boys sat on another bench. How many children are sitting on both benches?

   Add   Subtract

____ children

Superstar Students

Fill in the table using the information given. Then answer the questions.

Second Grade Students at Superstar School

Class	Boys	Girls	Total
A		17	28
B	12	15	
C	9		23
Total			

1. Which class has the most students? _____

2. Which class has the least students? _____

3. How many more girls than boys are in second grade? _____

4. Which class has the most boys? _____

5. Which class has the least girls? _____

6. If each boy in class A gave his teacher an apple, how many apples would she get? _____

7. How many students are in second grade at Superstar School? _____ Outline in red the box that tells this.

8. How many more students are in class A than class C? _____

9. If each boy in class B gave a girl in class A an apple, how many girls would not get an apple? _____

10. If 9 students move away, how many students would be in second grade then? _____

Tree Troubles

Help the squirrels get to their trees. Add or subtract in your head.
Write the final answer on the tree.

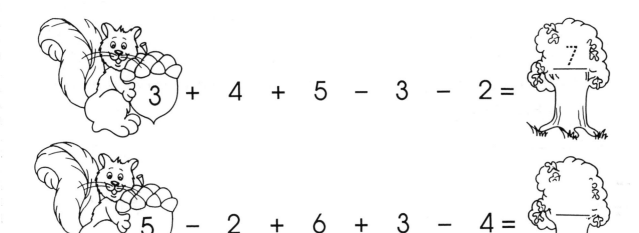

3 + 4 + 5 – 3 – 2 =

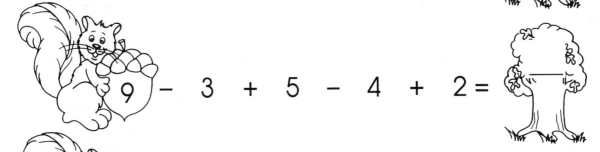

5 – 2 + 6 + 3 – 4 =

9 – 3 + 5 – 4 + 2 =

6 + 6 – 5 + 3 – 2 =

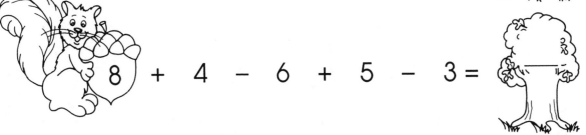

8 + 4 – 6 + 5 – 3 =

Roll Call

Look at the animals at the top of the page. Write the correct word to tell where each animal is standing in the line.

1. _____

2. _____

3. _____

4. _____

5. _____

6. _____

7. _____

8. _____

9. _____

10. _____

Word Bank

first
second
third
fourth
fifth
sixth
seventh
eighth
ninth
tenth

Name _____

My First Treat Will Be...

Circle the ordinal number word for each treat.

1.

2.

3.

4.

16.

5.

15.

6.

14.

7.

13.

8.

12.

11.

10.

9.

 third, sixteenth, (fifth)

 fifteenth, fourth, first

 twelfth, second, seventh

 third, eleventh, fifteenth

 eighth, first, tenth

 sixteenth, thirteenth, third

 ninth, second, thirteenth

 sixth, seventh, ninth,

Second Grade Bound © Carson-Dellosa • CD-704635

Who Has the Most?

Circle the right answer.

1.

Jane has 3 🐷's.
Bob has 4 🐷's.
Bill has 5 🐷's.

Who has the most 🐷's?

Jane   Bob   Bill

2.

Pam has 7 🐶's.
Joe has 5 🐶's.
Jane has 6 🐶's.

Who has the most 🐶's?

Pam   Joe   Jane

3.

Amy has 23 🐰's.

Sandy has 19 🐰's.

Jack has 25 🐰's.

Who has the most 🐰's?

Amy   Sandy   Jack

4.

Ann has 19 🐔's.

Burt has 18 🐔's.

Brent has 17 🐔's.

Who has the most 🐔's?

Ann   Burt   Brent

5.

The boys have 14 🐱's.
The girls have 16 🐱's.
The teachers have 17 🐱's.

Who has the most 🐱's?

boys   girls   teachers

6.

Rose has 12 🐄's.

Betsy has 11 🐄's.

Ann has 13 🐄's.

Who has the most 🐄's?

Rose   Betsy   Ann

Who Has the Least?

Circle the right answer.

1.

Pat had 4 🏈's.
Charles had 3 🏈's.
Jane had 5 🏈's.

Who had the least number of 🏈's?

Pat   Charles   Jane

2.

Jeff has 5 's.
John has 4 's.
Bill has 6 's.

Who has the least number of 's?

Jeff   John   Bill

3.

Jane has 7 ⚾'s.
Peg has 9 ⚾'s.
Fred has 8 ⚾'s.

Who has the least number of ⚾'s?

Jane   Peg   Fred

4.

Charles bought 12 's.
Rose bought 6 's.
Mother bought 24 's.

Who bought the least number of 's?

Charles   Rose   Mother

5.

John had 9 ⚽'s.
Jack had 8 ⚽'s.
Jeff had 7 ⚽'s.

Who had the least number of ⚽'s?

John   Jack   Jeff

6.

Alma bought 12 's.
Nina bought 16 's.
Marty bought 13 's.

Who bought the least number of 's?

Alma   Nina   Marty

Munch a Bunch

Gertrude Goat and her friends Ginger, George, and Gus are making special popcorn balls. Each piece of popcorn has a number on it.

Read the clues to find out which pieces of popcorn each goat will use for his or her popcorn ball. Write the numbers on the popcorn.

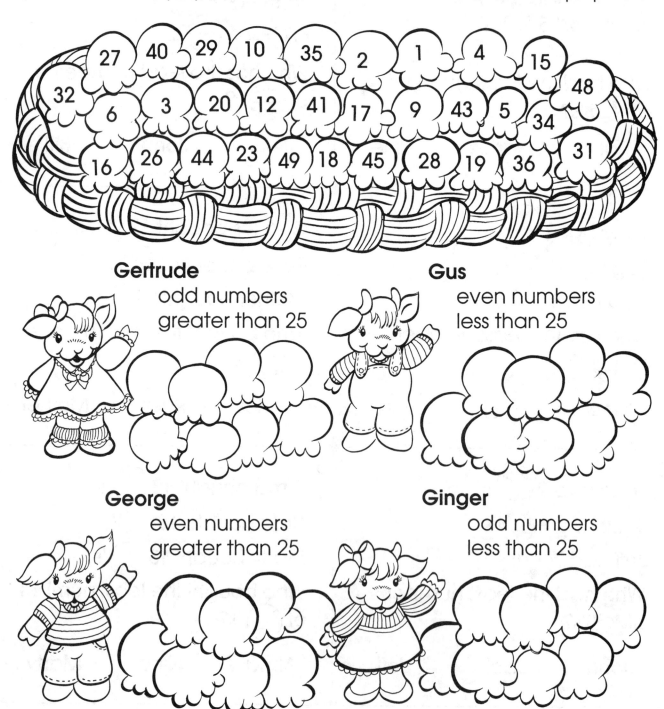

Gertrude
odd numbers
greater than 25

Gus
even numbers
less than 25

George
even numbers
greater than 25

Ginger
odd numbers
less than 25

Name ______________________

"Mouth" Math

Write < or > in each circle. Make sure the "mouth" is open toward the greater number!

36 ○ 49	35 ○ 53
20 ○ 18	74 ○ 21
53 ○ 76	68 ○ 80
29 ○ 26	45 ○ 19
90 ○ 89	70 ○ 67

Space Time

What time is it?

_____

_____

_____

_____

_____

_____

_____

_____

_____

_____

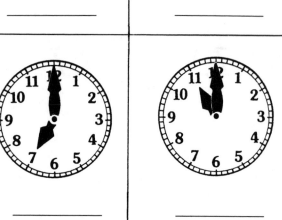
_____

_____

Right on Time

Cut out the time signs at the bottom of the page. Paste each sign on the engine next to the correct clock.

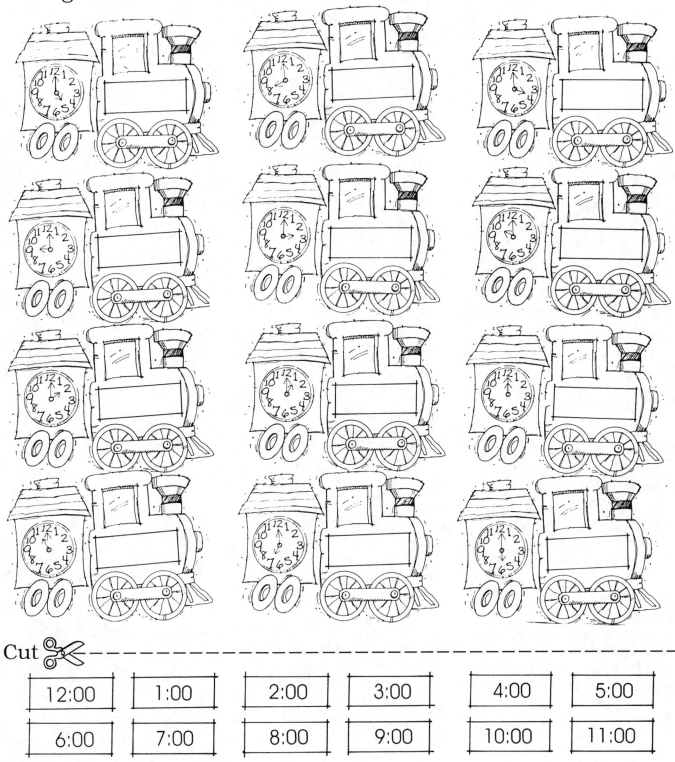

Cut ✂ -

12:00	1:00	2:00	3:00	4:00	5:00
6:00	7:00	8:00	9:00	10:00	11:00

Turtle Time

What time is it?

_____

_____

_____

_____

_____

_____

_____

_____

_____

_____

_____

Write the time.
Draw the hands on each clock.

I get up at_____.

I go to bed at_____.

School starts at_____.

I watch TV at_____.

Lunch is at_____.

Dinner is at_____.

Recess is at_____.   School ends at_____.   I play at_____.

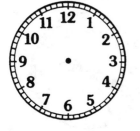

Time to Clean Up

Match the digital time with each clock face by cutting and pasting each lid on the correct trash can.

It's About Time

 Trace each 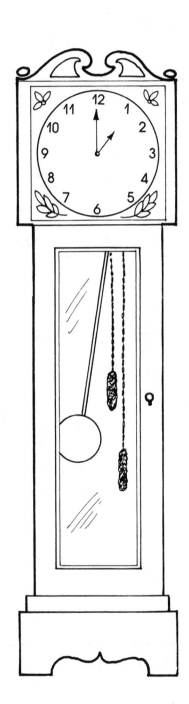 with red if it has a time word.

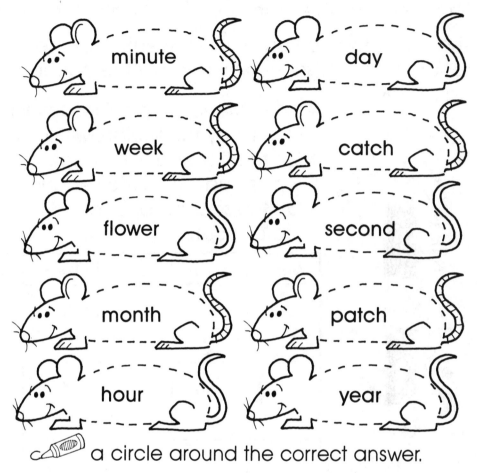

minute	day
week	catch
flower	second
month	patch
hour	year

a circle around the correct answer.

1. There are sixty seconds in a   minute.
     year.

2. There are sixty minutes in an   second.
     hour.

3. There are 24 hours in a   minute.
     day.

4. There are 365 days in a   year.
     week.

5. There are seven days in a   week.
     hour.

6. There are twelve months in a   year.
     week.

Weather Watch

Weather is the condition of the air around the earth for a period of time. The weatherman's job is to predict the weather.

There were some very unusual weather patterns recorded for a recent month. Use the key to draw the correct weather symbols for each day.

- Every Monday and Tuesday it rained. Then it was sunny for the following three days.
- On the first and third weekends, the first day was cloudy, and the second day was snowy.
- On the second and fourth weekends, it was just the opposite.

Key

sunny	☀
cloudy	☁
rainy	🌧
snowy	❄

Sun.	Mon.	Tues.	Wed.	Thurs.	Fri.	Sat.
		1	2	3	4	5
6	7	8	9	10	11	12
13	14	15	16	17	18	19
20	21	22	23	24	25	26
27	28	29	30	31		

Write the word that tells about the weather on these dates:

- 6th day of the month   _____
- 13th day of the month   _____
- last day of the month   _____

Postage Stamp, Please

Add up the coins on each envelope. Write the total on the stamp.

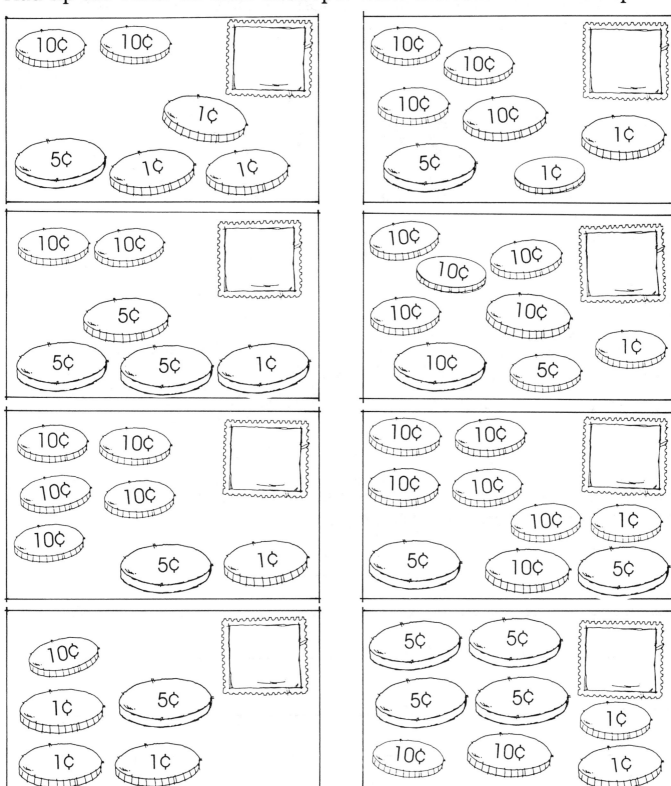

Pencil Topper Purchases

Peggy wants to buy three different pencil toppers. Look at the cost of each topper.

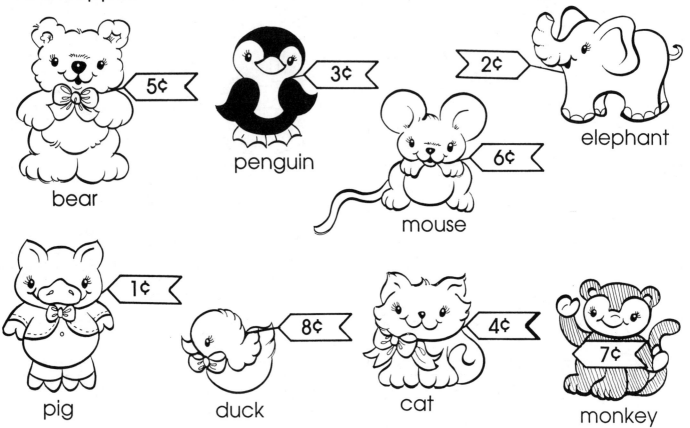

bear   5¢

penguin   3¢

mouse   6¢

2¢   elephant

pig   1¢

duck   8¢

cat   4¢

monkey   7¢

Peggy has 12¢ to spend. Write the names of the different pencil topper combinations she might pick.

1. _____   1. _____   1. _____

2. _____   2. _____   2. _____

3. _____   3. _____   3. _____

1. _____   1. _____   1. _____

2. _____   2. _____   2. _____

3. _____   3. _____   3. _____

Second Grade Bound © Carson-Dellosa • CD-704635

Mall Mania

Count the coins in each purse. Then draw a line from each coin purse to the store where that amount is given.

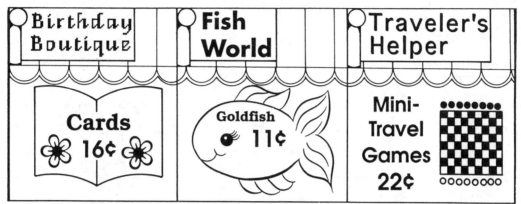

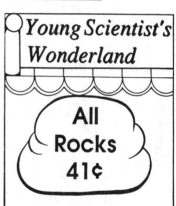

In which store did you not spend any money? _____

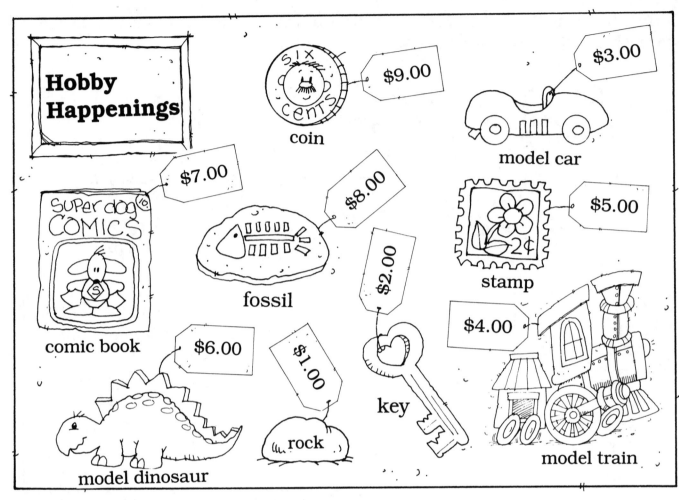

Hobby Happenings

coin — $9.00

model car — $3.00

comic book — $7.00

fossil — $8.00

stamp — $5.00

$2.00

model dinosaur — $6.00

rock — $1.00

key

model train — $4.00

You want to buy 3 **different** items in the hobby store. You have $16.00. Write all the different combinations of items you can buy using the entire $16.00.

1. _____   1. _____   1. _____   1. _____

2. _____   2. _____   2. _____   2. _____

3. _____   3. _____   3. _____   3. _____

1. _____   1. _____   1. _____   1. _____

2. _____   2. _____   2. _____   2. _____

3. _____   3. _____   3. _____   3. _____

Earnings Add Up!

Help Wanted

 Wash dishes $1.50

 Feed cat $.95

 Mow lawn $3.50

 Mop floors $1.25

 Pick tomatoes $2.75

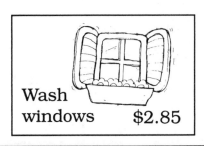 Wash windows $2.85

Use the Help Wanted poster above to help you find out how much you can earn by doing each set of jobs. Write the total amount for each set.

1. feed cat	1. wash dishes	1. wash windows	1. feed cat
2. pick tomatoes	2. mow lawn	2. mop floors	2. wash windows
3. wash dishes	3. wash windows	3. mow lawn	3. mop floors

1. pick tomatoes	1. feed cat	1. pick tomatoes	1. mop floors
2. wash windows	2. wash dishes	2. wash windows	2. pick tomatoes
3. feed cat	3. mop floors	3. mow lawn	3. wash windows

Here's Your Order

Count the money on each tray. Write the name of the food that costs that amount.

hamburger ..$2.45	milk ....$.64	cake $2.85
hot dog $1.77	soda pop $1.26	pie $2.25
sandwich $1.55	milkshake ...$1.89	sundae......$.95

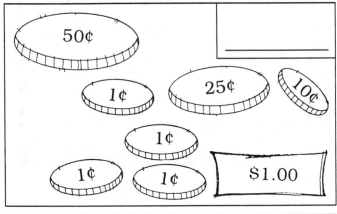

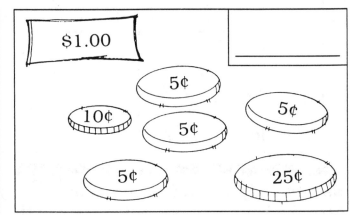

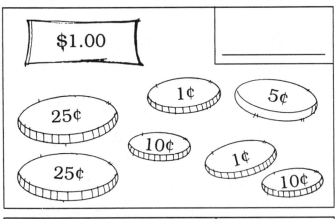

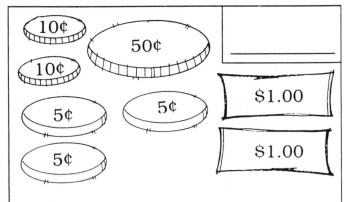

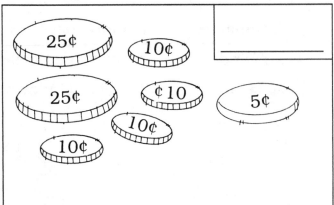

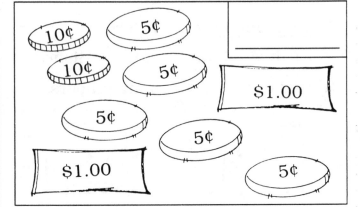

Flowers that "Measure" Up

Cut out the centimeter ruler at the bottom of the page. Use the ruler to measure how tall each flower is from the bottom of the stem to the top of the flower. Write the answer below the bee.

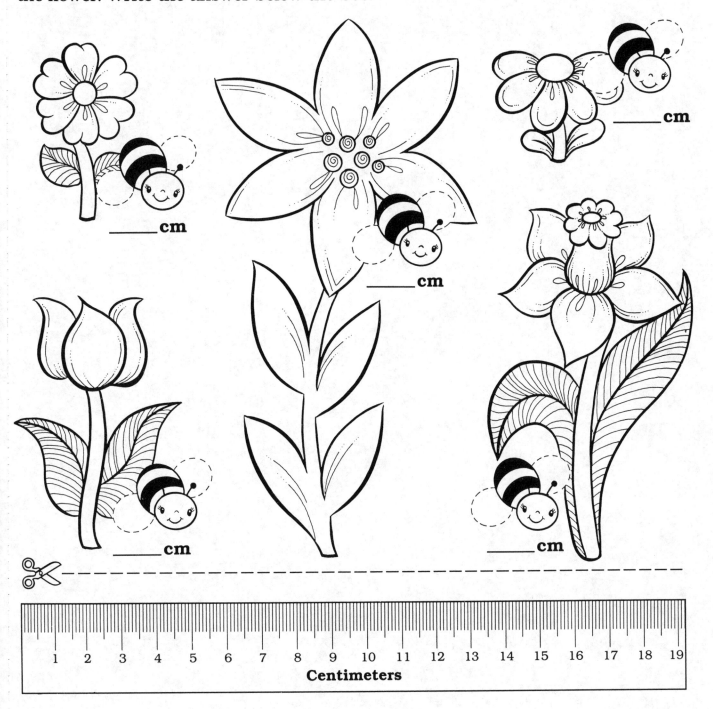

_____ cm

_____ cm

_____ cm

_____ cm

_____ cm

1 2 3 4 5 6 7 8 9 10 11 12 13 14 15 16 17 18 19

Centimeters

Brush Up on Measuring!

Use your centimeter ruler to measure these brushes to the nearest centimeter.

about _____ centimeters   about _____ centimeters

about _____ centimeters   about _____ centimeters

about _____ centimeters   about _____ centimeters

about _____ centimeters

about _____ centimeters   about _____ centimeters

about _____ centimeters

Jungle Journey

Use a centimeter ruler to measure the line segments. Write the total length on each hut.

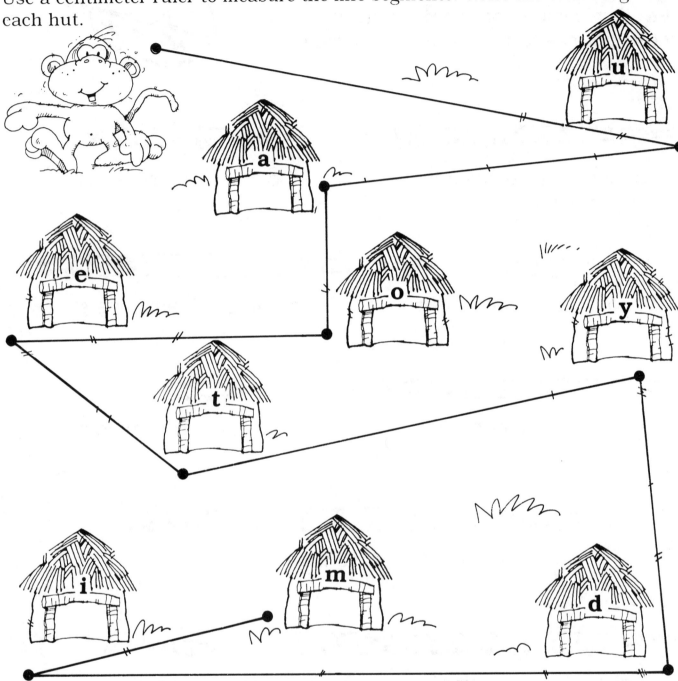

Use the numbers and the letters on the huts to solve the code.

___ ___ ___   ___ ___ ___ ___   ___ ___!
13 4 15   7 10 8 9   18 6

Second Grade Bound © Carson-Dellosa • CD-704635

Gauging the Weather

Cut out the centimeter ruler at the bottom of the page. Use the ruler to measure the amount of rainfall from the bottom of the gauge to the top of the water. Write the measurement on the raindrop.

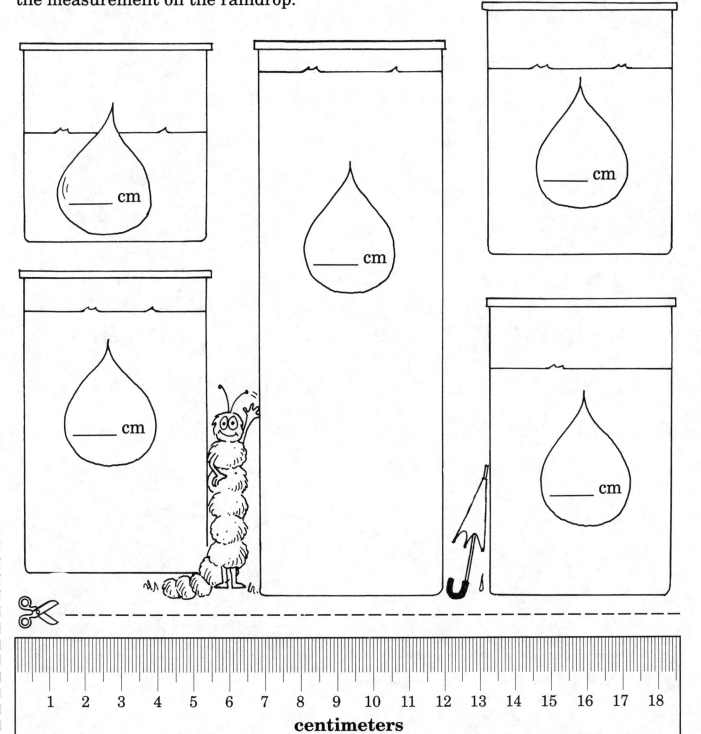

Jumping Jellybeans

Use an inch ruler to measure the line segments. Write the total length on each candy jar.

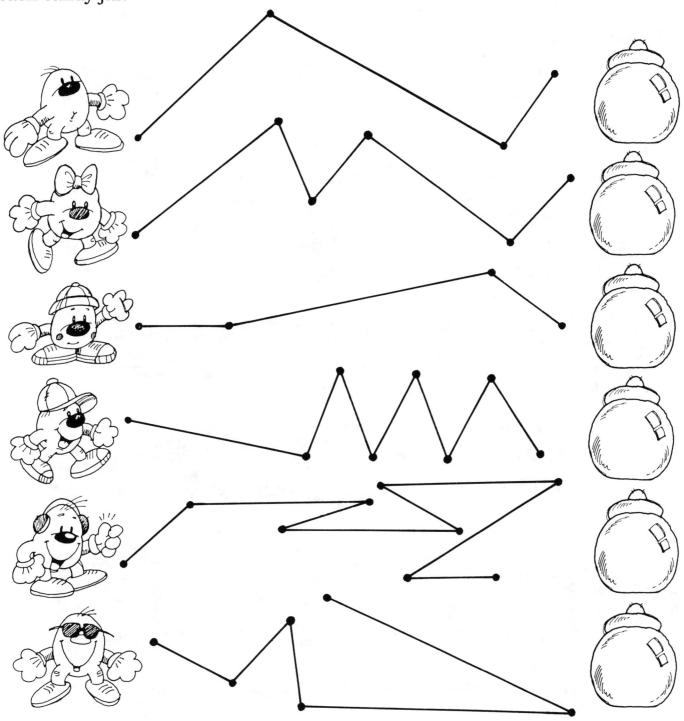

Measure these worms to the nearest inch.

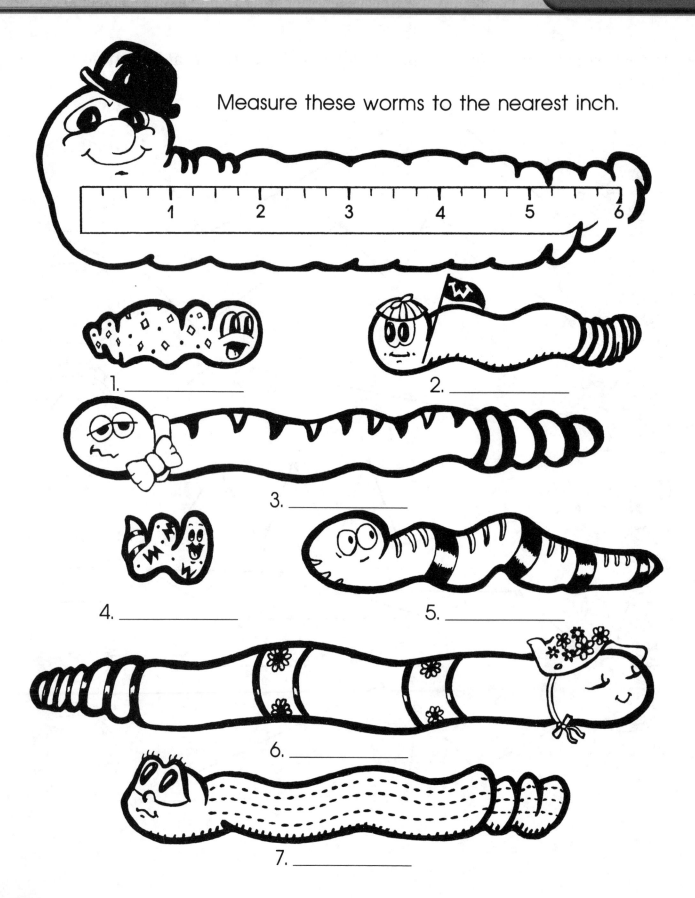

1. _____

2. _____

3. _____

4. _____

5. _____

6. _____

7. _____

How Big Are You?

You are getting so big! Every day, you grow a little more. Estimate how long some of your body parts are. Then, using a ruler, work with a friend to find the actual measurements.

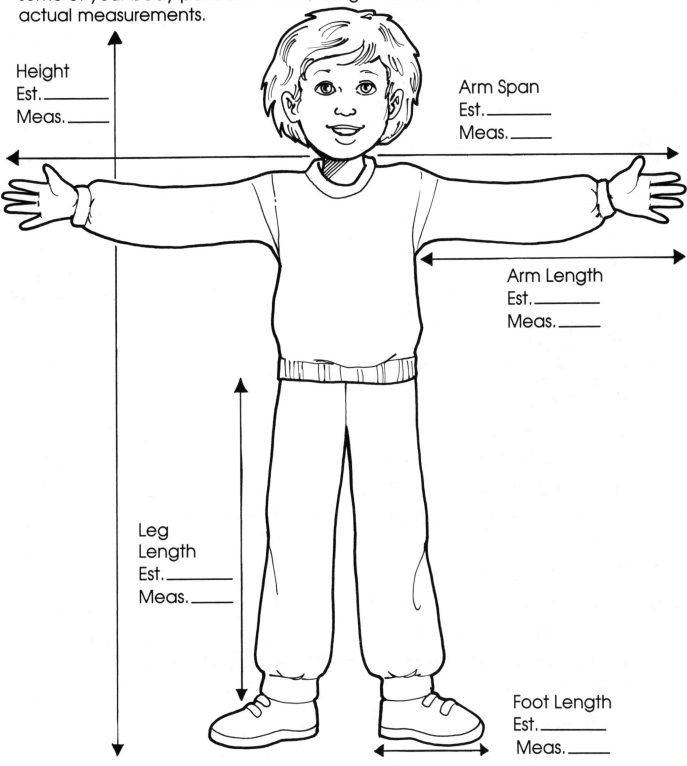

Height
Est. _____
Meas. _____

Arm Span
Est. _____
Meas. _____

Arm Length
Est. _____
Meas. _____

Leg
Length
Est. _____
Meas. _____

Foot Length
Est. _____
Meas. _____

How Far Is It?

Use your ruler to measure each distance on the map. Then use the letters on the tires and your answers to solve the message at the bottom of the page.

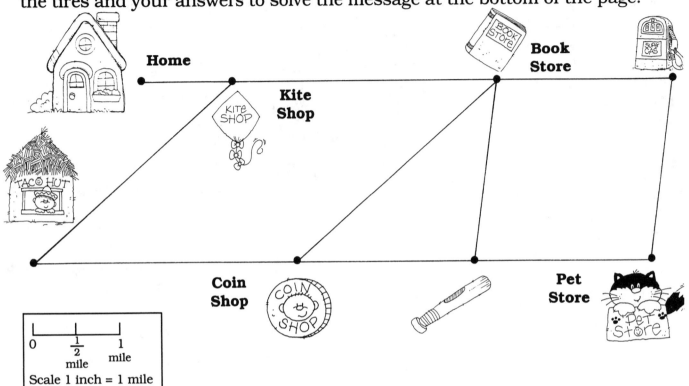

Scale 1 inch = 1 mile

How far is it from . . .

1. home to the Kite Shop? _____ (s)

2. home to the Book Store to the Gas Station? _____ (e)

3. home to the Kite Shop to the Taco Hut? _____ (p)

4. the Taco Hut to the Coin Shop to the Book Store to the Gas Station? _____ (a)

5. the Taco Hut to the Coin Shop? _____ (u)

6. the Baseball Field to the Book Store to the Kite Shop? _____ (d)

7. the Pet Store to the Gas Station? _____ (r)

8. the Gas Station to the Pet Store to the Baseball Field to the Coin Shop to the Taco Hut? _____ (m)

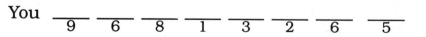

You __ __ __ __ __ __ __ __   __ __ !
   9 6 8 1 3 2 6 5   3 4

Second Grade Bound © Carson-Dellosa • CD-704635

Name _____

Draw a line from the containers on the left to the containers on the right that will hold the same amount of liquid. **Hint:** 2 pints = 1 quart.

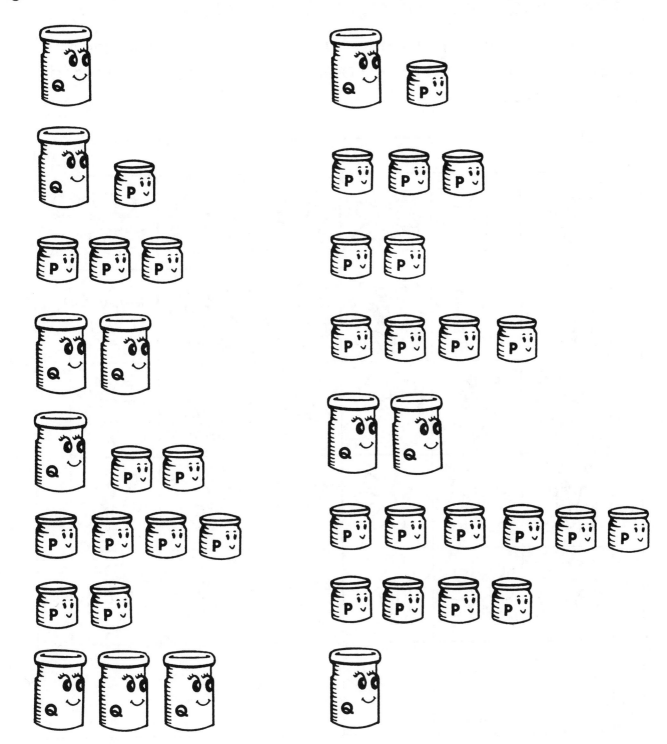

Sew What?

A favorite activity of colonial women and girls was getting together for a quilting bee. The quilts, made from scraps of linen, wool, and cotton, were frequently sewn together in a pattern.

Look carefully at the pattern in the unfinished quilt below. Then continue the pattern by drawing pictures in the blank sections to complete the quilt.

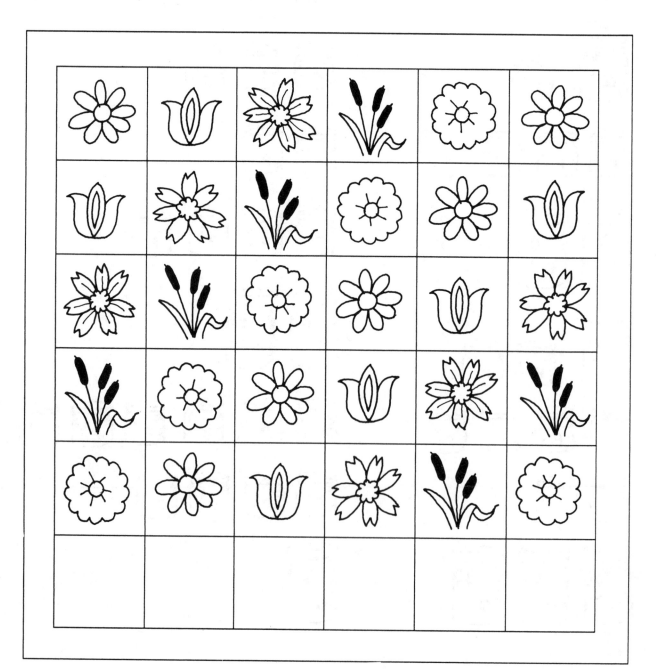

Shape Sort

Color the ones in each row that are the same size and shape. Write **T** for triangle, **R** for rectangle and **S** for square.

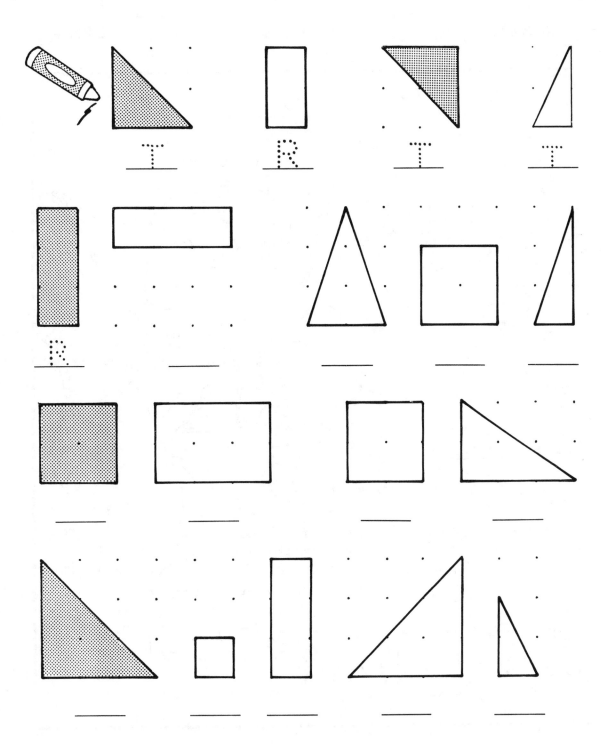

Sea Shapes

Find the shapes and color them using the code.

△ red   ◯ blue   ◇ yellow

⬭ green   ⬜ orange   ▭ black

Equal and Unequal Parts

Cut out each shape below along the solid lines. Then fold the shape on the dotted lines. Do you get equal or unequal parts? Sort the shapes into two piles: those with equal parts and those with unequal parts.

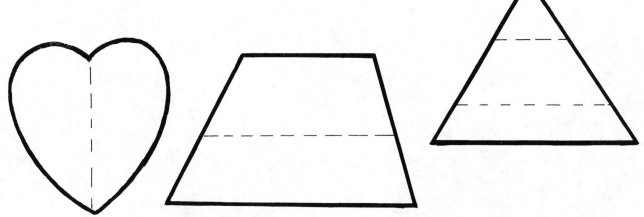

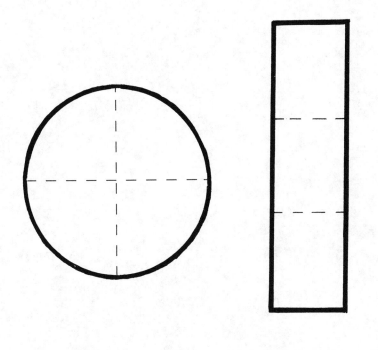

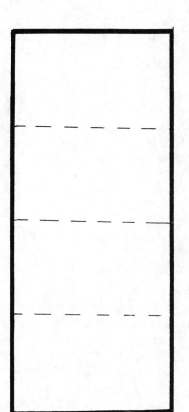

Shaded Shapes

Draw line from fraction to correct shape.

$\dfrac{1}{3}$ shaded

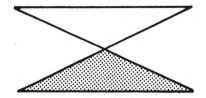

$\dfrac{2}{4}$ shaded

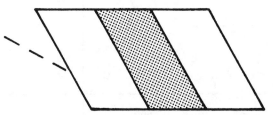

$\dfrac{1}{4}$ shaded

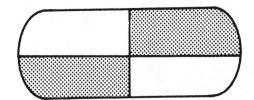

$\dfrac{1}{2}$ shaded

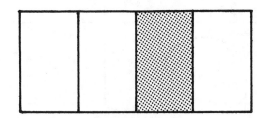

$\dfrac{3}{4}$ shaded

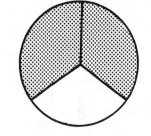

$\dfrac{2}{3}$ shaded

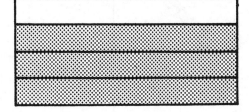

Fraction Food

Count the equal parts. Circle the fraction that names one of the parts.

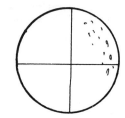

$\frac{1}{2}$ $\frac{1}{3}$ $\frac{1}{4}$

$\frac{1}{2}$ $\frac{1}{3}$ $\frac{1}{4}$

$\frac{1}{2}$ $\frac{1}{3}$ $\frac{1}{4}$

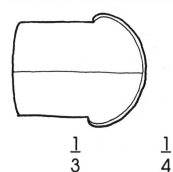

$\frac{1}{2}$ $\frac{1}{3}$ $\frac{1}{4}$

$\frac{1}{2}$ $\frac{1}{3}$ $\frac{1}{4}$

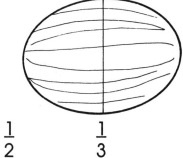

$\frac{1}{2}$ $\frac{1}{3}$ $\frac{1}{4}$

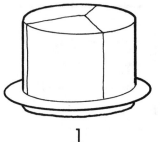

$\frac{1}{2}$ $\frac{1}{3}$ $\frac{1}{4}$

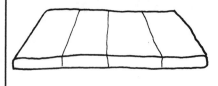

$\frac{1}{2}$ $\frac{1}{3}$ $\frac{1}{4}$

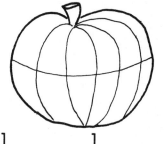

$\frac{1}{2}$ $\frac{1}{3}$ $\frac{1}{4}$

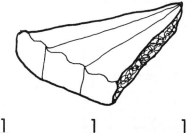

$\frac{1}{2}$ $\frac{1}{3}$ $\frac{1}{4}$

$\frac{1}{2}$ $\frac{1}{3}$ $\frac{1}{4}$

$\frac{1}{2}$ $\frac{1}{3}$ $\frac{1}{4}$

Second Grade Bound © Carson-Dellosa • CD-704635

Fortunate Fractions

Read the fraction on each tray. Color the correct number of fortune cookies to show each fraction.

Turtle Spots

Count the spots on the turtles.
Color the boxes to show how many spots.

1	2	3	4	5	6	7	8

Name _____

Wormy Apples

Color the boxes to show how many worms.
Answer the questions.

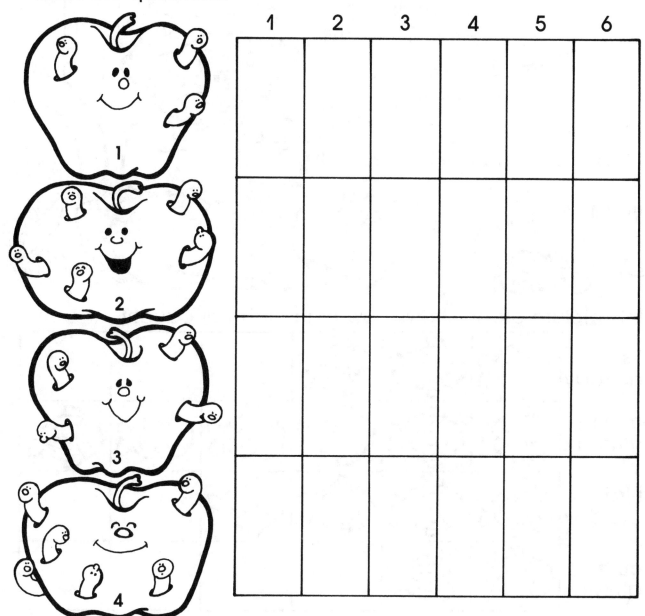

	1	2	3	4	5	6

How many worms in apple 1? ___ 2? ___ 3? ___ 4? ___

In apples 1 and 3? ___ In apples 2 and 4? ___

How many more worms in apple 4 than in apple 2? ___

How many more worms in apple 3 than in apple 1? ___

Pat's Fish

This picture graph shows how many fish Pat caught.

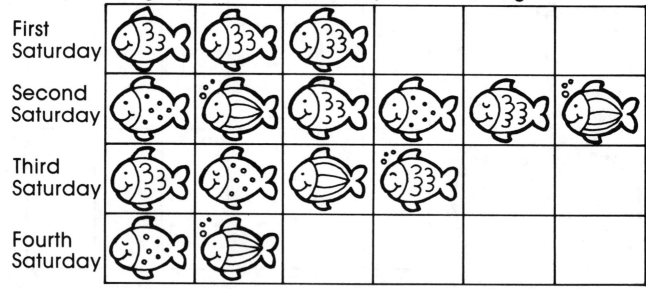

Color the fish Pat caught on the third Saturday **red**.
Color the fish he caught on the first Saturday **blue**.
the second Saturday **yellow**, and the fourth Saturday **green**.
How many fish did he catch on the first Saturday? ____
second Saturday? ____ third Saturday? ____ fourth Saturday? ____

Honey Bear's Bakery

Look at the picture of the bakery. Fill in the graph to show how many of each treat are in the picture.

Number of Bakery Treats

12						
11						
10						
9						
8						
7						
6						
5						
4						
3						
2						
1						
0						

Treasure Quest

Read the directions. Draw the pictures where they belong on the grid.

Start at 0 and go . . .

over 2, up 5. Draw a

over 9, up 3. Draw a

over 8, up 6. Draw a

over 5, up 2. Draw a

over 1, up 7. Draw a

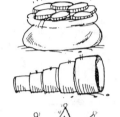

over 7, up 1. Draw a

over 6, up 4. Draw a

over 2, up 3. Draw a

over 3, up 1. Draw a

over 4, up 6. Draw a

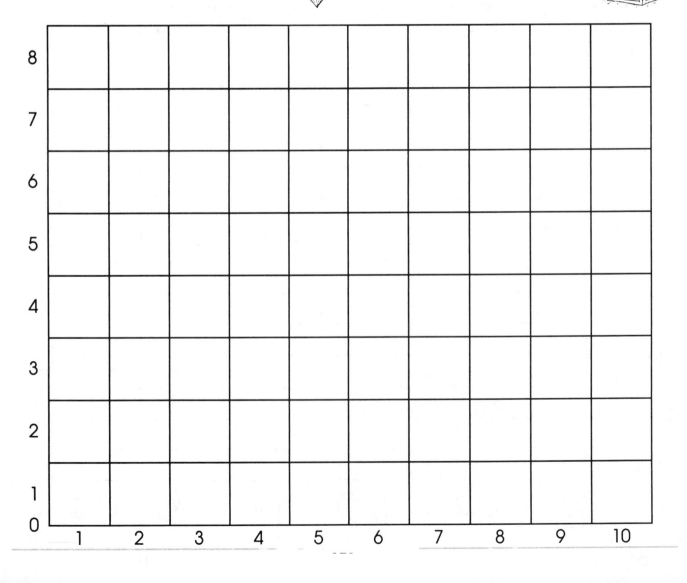

Second Grade Bound © Carson-Dellosa • CD-704635

Multiplying Rabbits

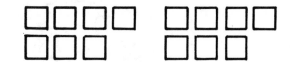

7 + 7 = __14__
2 sevens = ____
2 × 7 = ____

___8___ + ___8___ = __16__
2 eights = ____
2 × ___8___ = ____

2 + 2 + 2 + 2 = _____
____twos = ____
____ × 2 = ____

3 + 3 + 3 + 3 + 3 = _____
____threes = ____
____ × 3 = ____

4 + 4 + 4 = _____
____fours = ____
____ × 4 = ____

9 + 9 = _____
2 nines = ____
____ × 9 = ____

5 + 5 + 5 = _____
____fives = ____
____ × 5 = ____

6 + 6 = _____
____sixes = ____
____ × 6 = ____

3 + 3 + 3 + 3 = _____
____threes = ____
____ × 3 = ____

4 + 4 = _____
____fours = ____
____ × 4 = ____

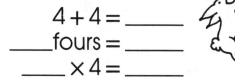

Mr. X and His Cookies

Draw a line from each picture to its matching problem.

$4 \times 3 = 12$

$3 \times 3 = 9$

$2 \times 9 = 18$

$4 \times 4 = 16$

$3 \times 6 = 18$

$3 \times 5 = 15$

$5 \times 2 = 10$

Second Grade Bound © Carson-Dellosa • CD-704635

Amazing Amphibians

Amphibians are cold-blooded vertebrates (animals with backbones). They have no scales on their skin. Most amphibians hatch from eggs laid in water or on damp ground. Many amphibians grow legs as they develop into adults. Some live on land and have both lungs and gills for breathing. Frogs and toads are examples of amphibians.

Santjie, a South African sharp-nosed frog, holds the record for the longest triple jump. He jumped a total of more than 33 feet!

The frogs below won 1st, 2nd, and 3rd place in a recent triple-jump contest. Each jump after each frog's first jump was two feet shorter than the jump before. How many total feet did each frog jump? Fill in the answers on the trophies.

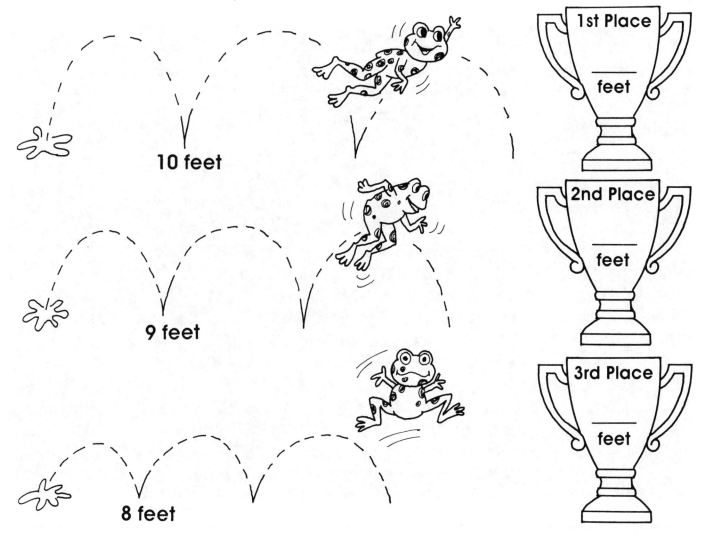

10 feet

9 feet

8 feet

1st Place
_____ feet

2nd Place
_____ feet

3rd Place
_____ feet

Math Checklist

Read the following skills aloud. Ask your child to place a check mark in each box once he or she has mastered the second grade skill.

- ☐ Counting
- ☐ Skip Counting
- ☐ Addition
- ☐ Subtraction
- ☐ Regrouping
- ☐ Problem Solving
- ☐ Estimation
- ☐ Ordinal Numbers
- ☐ Comparing Numbers

- ☐ Time
- ☐ Money
- ☐ Measurement
- ☐ Volume
- ☐ Patterns
- ☐ Geometry
- ☐ Fractions
- ☐ Graphing
- ☐ Multiplication

Now, try these fun learning activities!

Try these hands-on activities for enhancing your child's learning and development. Be sure to encourage speaking, listening, touching, and active movement.

- Say or write word problems for your child that include a missing number. For example, ask, "I had __ books. I read 4 books. I have 2 left to read. What number is missing?" or "I had 10 grapes. I ate ___ grapes. I had 7 left. What number is missing?"

- Make several flash cards to practice greater than and less than. On two index cards, write < and >. On several other cards, write a one- or two-digit number, one number per card. Then, have your child randomly choose two numbers, placing the correct < or > card between them.

- Make a tactile graph from actual objects organized in equally spaced columns. Choose a collection of small objects, such as marbles or buttons. Have your child sort the collection into groups and name each group. Then, write the group names at the bottom of a grid drawn on a large sheet of paper (with individual boxes large enough to hold a piece of the collection). Above each name, have your child line up the group, one object per box. Discuss the graph and answer questions about the information it shows.

Second Grade Bound © Carson-Dellosa • CD-704635

Answer Key

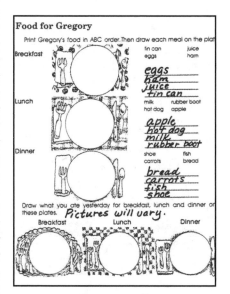

Food for Gregory

Print Gregory's food in ABC order. Then draw each meal on the plate.

Breakfast
tin can   juice
eggs   ham

eggs
ham
juice
tin can

Lunch
milk   rubber boot
hot dog   apple

apple
hot dog
milk
rubber boot

Dinner
shoe   fish
carrots   bread

bread
carrots
fish
shoe

Draw what you ate yesterday for breakfast, lunch and dinner on these plates. *Pictures will vary.*

Breakfast   Lunch   Dinner

Page 10

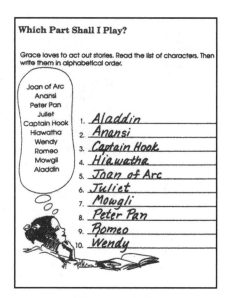

Which Part Shall I Play?

Grace loves to act out stories. Read the list of characters. Then write them in alphabetical order.

Joan of Arc
Anansi
Peter Pan
Juliet
Captain Hook
Hiawatha
Wendy
Romeo
Mowgli
Aladdin

1. *Aladdin*
2. *Anansi*
3. *Captain Hook*
4. *Hiawatha*
5. *Joan of Arc*
6. *Juliet*
7. *Mowgli*
8. *Peter Pan*
9. *Romeo*
10. *Wendy*

Page 11

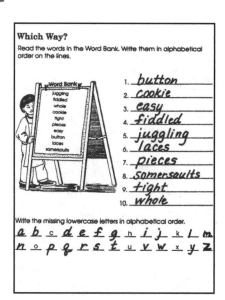

Which Way?

Read the words in the Word Bank. Write them in alphabetical order on the lines.

Word Bank
juggling
fiddled
whole
cookie
tight
pieces
easy
button
laces
somersaults

1. *button*
2. *cookie*
3. *easy*
4. *fiddled*
5. *juggling*
6. *laces*
7. *pieces*
8. *somersaults*
9. *tight*
10. *whole*

Write the missing lowercase letters in alphabetical order.

a b *c* d e f *g* h i *j* k l *m*
n *o* p *q* r *s* t *u* v *w* x *y* z

Page 12

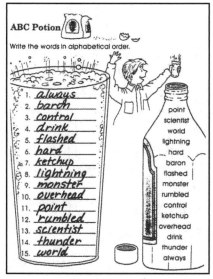

ABC Potion

Write the words in alphabetical order.

1. *always*
2. *baron*
3. *control*
4. *drink*
5. *flashed*
6. *hard*
7. *ketchup*
8. *lightning*
9. *monster*
10. *overhead*
11. *point*
12. *rumbled*
13. *scientist*
14. *thunder*
15. *world*

point
scientist
world
lightning
hard
baron
flashed
monster
rumbled
control
ketchup
overhead
drink
thunder
always

Page 13

Crazy Creatures

Draw a line to each letter in ABC order to finish this dot-to-dot picture.

Now color and add details to the picture. Then write all the consonants in order on these lines.

1. *b*   5. *g*   9. *m*   13. *q*   17. *v*   21. *z*
2. *c*   6. *h*   10. *m*   14. *r*   18. *w*
3. *d*   7. *j*   11. *n*   15. *s*   19. *x*
4. *f*   8. *k*   12. *p*   16. *t*   20. *y*

Page 14

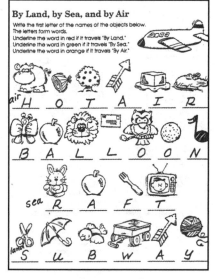

By Land, by Sea, and by Air

Write the first letter of the names of the objects below. The letters form words.
Underline the word in red if it travels "By Land."
Underline the word in green if it travels "By Sea."
Underline the word in orange if it travels "By Air."

air   H O T A I R

B A L L O O N

sea   R A F T

land   S U B W A Y

Page 15

Answer Key

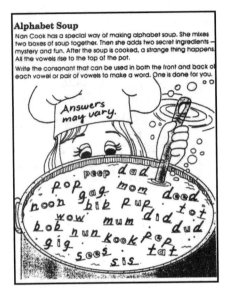

Alphabet Soup

Nan Cook has a special way of making alphabet soup. She mixes two boxes of soup together. Then she adds two secret ingredients — mystery and fun. After the soup is cooked, a strange thing happens. All the vowels rise to the top of the pot.

Write the consonant that can be used in both the front and back of each vowel or pair of vowels to make a word. One is done for you.

Page 16

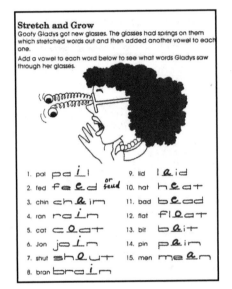

Stretch and Grow

Goofy Gladys got new glasses. The glasses had springs on them which stretched words out and then added another vowel to each one.

Add a vowel to each word below to see what words Gladys saw through her glasses.

1. pal — pail
2. fed — feed or feud
3. chin — chain
4. ran — rain
5. cat — coat
6. Jon — join
7. shut — shout
8. bran — brain
9. lid — laid
10. hat — heat
11. bad — bead
12. flat — float
13. bit — bait
14. pin — pain
15. men — mean

Page 17

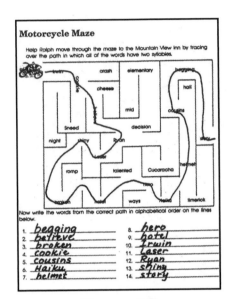

Motorcycle Maze

Help Ralph move through the maze to the Mountain View Inn by tracing over the path in which all of the words have two syllables.

Now write the words from the correct path in alphabetical order on the lines below.

1. begging
2. believe
3. broken
4. cookie
5. cousins
6. Haiku
7. helmet
8. hero
9. hotel
10. Irwin
11. laser
12. Ryan
13. shiny
14. story

Page 18

Trick or Treat Syllables

Think about how many syllables are in each word in the Word Bank. Then write each word on the correct jack-o'-lantern.

1 Syllable
voice
clothes
masks
ghost

2 Syllables
pirate
spooky
costume
princess

3 Syllables
invited
faraway
Halloween
apartment

4 Syllables
elevator
escalator
anybody
evaporate

Word Bank

voice	elevator	costume	Halloween
clothes	pirate	faraway	anybody
masks	spooky	princess	apartment
invited	ghost	escalator	evaporate

Page 19

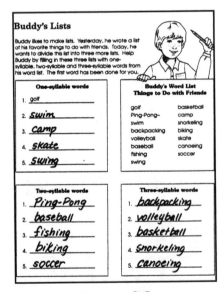

Buddy's Lists

Buddy likes to make lists. Yesterday, he wrote a list of his favorite things to do with friends. Today, he wants to divide this list into three more lists. Help Buddy by filling in these three lists with one-syllable, two-syllable and three-syllable words from his word list. The first word has been done for you.

One-syllable words
1. golf
2. swim
3. camp
4. skate
5. swing

Buddy's Word List
Things to Do with Friends

golf
Ping-Pong
swim
backpacking
volleyball
baseball
fishing
swing
basketball
camp
snorkeling
biking
skate
canoeing
soccer

Two-syllable words
1. Ping-Pong
2. baseball
3. fishing
4. biking
5. soccer

Three-syllable words
1. backpacking
2. volleyball
3. basketball
4. snorkeling
5. canoeing

Page 20

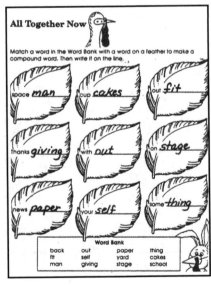

All Together Now

Match a word in the Word Bank with a word on a feather to make a compound word. Then write it on the line.

space man — cup cakes — out fit
Thanks giving — with out — on stage
news paper — your self — some thing

Word Bank

back	out	paper	thing
fit	self	yard	cakes
man	giving	stage	school

Page 21

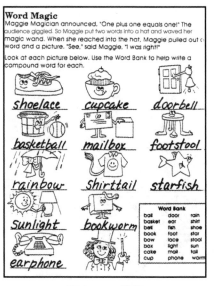

Word Magic

Maggie Magician announced, "One plus one equals one!" The audience giggled. So Maggie put two words into a hat and waved her magic wand. When she reached into the hat, Maggie pulled out a word and a picture. "See," said Maggie, "I was right!"

Look at each picture below. Use the Word Bank to help write a compound word for each.

shoelace cupcake doorbell
basketball mailbox footstool
rainbow shirttail starfish
sunlight bookworm
earphone

Word Bank
ball basket bell book bow box cake cup door ear fish foot lace light mail phone rain shirt shoe star stool sun tail worm

Page 22

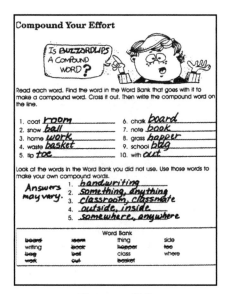

Compound Your Effort

Is BUZZARDLIPS A COMPOUND WORD?

Read each word. Find the word in the Word Bank that goes with it to make a compound word. Cross it out. Then write the compound word on the line.

1. coat **room**
2. snow **ball**
3. home **work**
4. waste **basket**
5. tip **toe**
6. chalk **board**
7. note **book**
8. grass **hopper**
9. school **bag**
10. with **out**

Look at the words in the Word Bank you did not use. Use those words to make your own compound words.

Answers may vary.
1. handwriting
2. something, anything
3. classroom, classmate
4. outside, inside
5. somewhere, anywhere

Word Bank
board writing bag room book bell out thing hopper class basket side toe where

Page 23

Mystery Word Mix-Up

Put on your detective hat! How many words can you make using only the letters in the words:

Nate the Great

1. neat
2. net
3. eat
4. ate
5. gate
6. get
7. treat
8. teeth
9. tea
10. green
11. ten
12. tan
13. teen
14. hear
15. heart
16. ear
17. gear
18. near
19. tear
20. greet
21. nag
22. tag

Others possible.

Page 24

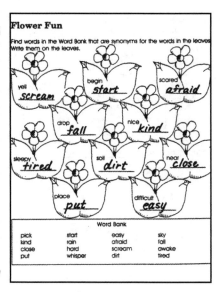

Flower Fun

Find words in the Word Bank that are synonyms for the words in the leaves. Write them on the leaves.

yell **scream**
begin **start**
scared **afraid**
drop **fall**
nice **kind**
sleepy **tired**
soil **dirt**
near **close**
place **put**
difficult **easy**

Word Bank
pick kind close put start rain hard whisper easy afraid scream dirt sky fall awake tired

Page 25

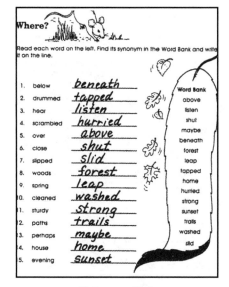

Where?

Read each word on the left. Find its synonym in the Word Bank and write it on the line.

1. below **beneath**
2. drummed **tapped**
3. hear **listen**
4. scrambled **hurried**
5. over **above**
6. close **shut**
7. slipped **slid**
8. woods **forest**
9. spring **leap**
10. cleaned **washed**
11. sturdy **strong**
12. paths **trails**
13. perhaps **maybe**
14. house **home**
15. evening **sunset**

Word Bank
above listen shut maybe beneath forest leap tapped home hurried strong sunset trails washed slid

Page 26

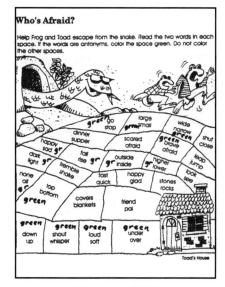

Who's Afraid?

Help Frog and Toad escape from the snake. Read the two words in each space. If the words are antonyms, color the space green. Do not color the other spaces.

Toad's House

Page 27

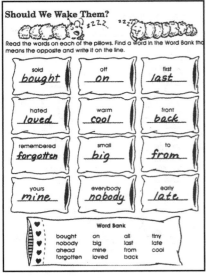

Should We Wake Them?

Read the words on each of the pillows. Find a word in the Word Bank that means the opposite and write it on the line.

sold	off	first
bought	*on*	*last*

hated	warm	front
loved	*cool*	*back*

remembered	small	to
forgotten	*big*	*from*

yours	everybody	early
mine	*nobody*	*late*

Word Bank

bought	on	all	tiny
nobody	big	last	late
ahead	mine	from	cool
forgotten	loved	back	

Page 28

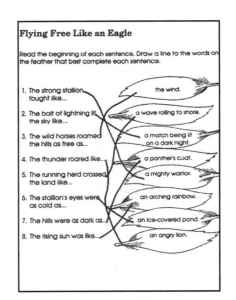

Flying Free Like an Eagle

Read the beginning of each sentence. Draw a line to the words on the feather that best complete each sentence.

1. The strong stallion fought like...
2. The bolt of lightning lit the sky like...
3. The wild horses roamed the hills as free as...
4. The thunder roared like...
5. The running herd crossed the land like...
6. The stallion's eyes were as cold as...
7. The hills were as dark as...
8. The rising sun was like...

the wind.
a wave rolling to shore.
a match being lit on a dark night.
a panther's coat.
a mighty warrior.
an arching rainbow.
an ice-covered pond.
an angry lion.

Page 29

Rain, Rain Go Away!

Read the naming parts in the tent. ___ one of the naming parts to begin each sentence.

Rain
Black clouds
A big wind
The campfire
Todd and Clint
The old green tent

1. *Todd and Clint* went camping.
2. *The old green tent* was hard to set up.
3. *A big wind* blew the trees.
4. *Black clouds* filled the sky.
5. *Rain* ran off the tent.
6. *The campfire* went out.

Page 30

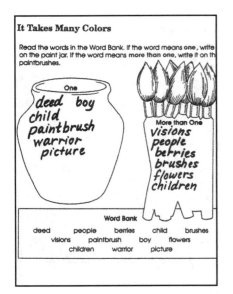

It Takes Many Colors

Read the words in the Word Bank. If the word means one, write on the paint jar. If the word means more than one, write it on th paintbrushes.

One
*deed boy
child
paintbrush
warrior
picture*

More than One
*visions
people
berries
brushes
flowers
children*

Word Bank

deed	people	berries	child	brushes
visions	paintbrush		boy	flowers
children	warrior		picture	

Page 31

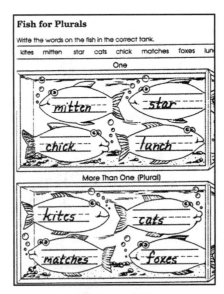

Fish for Plurals

Write the words on the fish in the correct tank.

kites mitten star cats chick matches foxes lun

One
*mitten star
chick lunch*

More Than One (Plural)
*kites cats
matches foxes*

Page 32

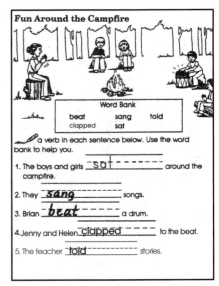

Fun Around the Campfire

Word Bank

beat	sang	told
clapped	sat	

___ a verb in each sentence below. Use the word bank to help you.

1. The boys and girls *sat* around the campfire.
2. They *sang* songs.
3. Brian *beat* a drum.
4. Jenny and Helen *clapped* to the beat.
5. The teacher *told* stories.

Page 33

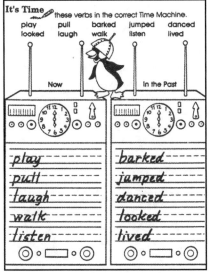

Page 34

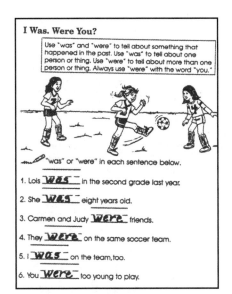

Page 35

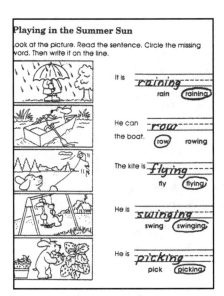

Page 36

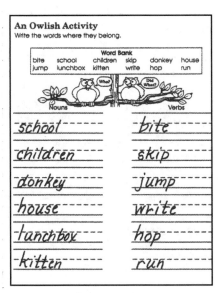

Page 37

Page 38

Page 39

Answer Key

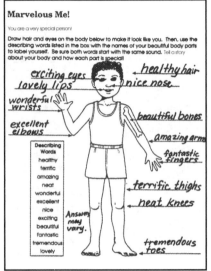

Marvelous Me!

You are a very special person!

Draw hair and eyes on the body below to make it look like you. Then, use the describing words listed in the box with the names of your beautiful body parts to label yourself. Be sure both words start with the same sound. Tell a story about your body and how each part is special!

- healthy hair
- exciting eyes
- nice nose
- lovely lips
- wonderful wrists
- beautiful bones
- excellent elbows
- amazing arms
- fantastic fingers
- terrific thighs
- neat knees
- tremendous toes

Describing Words: healthy, terrific, amazing, neat, wonderful, excellent, nice, exciting, beautiful, fantastic, tremendous, lovely

Answers may vary.

Page 40

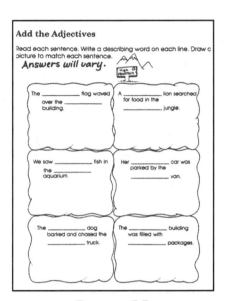

Add the Adjectives

Read each sentence. Write a describing word on each line. Draw a picture to match each sentence.

Answers will vary.

The _____ flag waved over the _____ building.

A _____ lion searched for food in the _____ jungle.

We saw _____ fish in the _____ aquarium.

Her _____ car was parked by the _____ van.

The _____ dog barked and chased the _____ truck.

The _____ building was filled with _____ packages.

Page 41

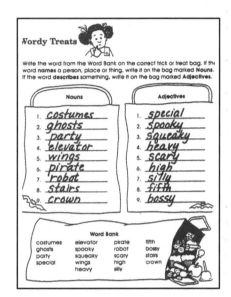

Wordy Treats

Write the word from the Word Bank on the correct trick or treat bag. If the word **names** a person, place or thing, write it on the bag marked **Nouns**. If the word **describes** something, write it on the bag marked **Adjectives**.

Nouns	Adjectives
1. costumes	1. special
2. ghosts	2. spooky
3. party	3. squeaky
4. elevator	4. heavy
5. wings	5. scary
6. pirate	6. high
7. robot	7. silly
8. stairs	8. fifth
9. crown	9. bossy

Word Bank

costumes, ghosts, party, special, elevator, spooky, squeaky, wings, heavy, pirate, robot, scary, high, silly, fifth, bossy, stairs, crown

Page 42

Summer Camp

A telling sentence begins with a capital letter and ends with a period. Write each telling sentence correctly on the lines.

Camp Rules

1. everyone goes to breakfast at 6:30 each morning

   Everyone goes to breakfast at 6:30 each morning.

2. only three people can ride in one canoe

   Only three people can ride in one canoe.

3. each person must help clean the cabins

   Each person must help clean the cabins.

4. older campers should help younger campers

   Older campers should help younger campers.

5. all lights are out by 9:00 each night

   All lights are out by 9:00 each night.

6. everyone should write home at least once a week

   Everyone should write home at least once a week.

Page 43

Tell-a-vision

Look at each TV picture. Write a telling sentence about each program. Answers will vary.

Page 44

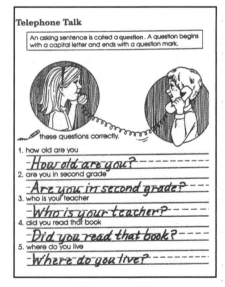

Telephone Talk

An asking sentence is called a question. A question begins with a capital letter and ends with a question mark.

_____ these questions correctly.

1. how old are you

   How old are you?

2. are you in second grade

   Are you in second grade?

3. who is your teacher

   Who is your teacher?

4. did you read that book

   Did you read that book?

5. where do you live

   Where do you live?

Page 45

Second Grade Bound © Carson-Dellosa • CD-704635

Asking Questions

Look at the picture. Write five asking sentences about the picture.

Answers will vary.

Page 46

That Doesn't Make Sense!

A sentence must make sense. Read each sentence. Put an X on the two words which do not belong. Write the corrected sentence on the lines below.

Yard Sale My neighbor is ~~orange~~ having a yard ~~very~~ sale.

1. *My neighbor is having a yard sale.*

She is ~~snow~~ selling lots of old things ~~phone.~~

2. *She is selling lots of old things.*

A man ~~until~~ is buying five ~~candle~~ old books.

3. *A man is buying five old books.*

My brother is buying an ~~salt~~ old checkers ~~X~~ game.

4. *My brother is buying an old checkers game.*

Two ladies ~~pull~~ are buying an old ~~touch~~ toy chest.

5. *Two ladies are buying an old toy chest.*

Page 47

Flight to Fun

Would you like to fly away for a fun trip? Write words about a trip on the plane. Use the words to write five sentences about the trip.

1. *Answers will vary.*
2. _____
3. _____
4. _____
5. _____

Page 48

About Me

Sentences can tell much about you. Begin at the START sign and write sentences that tell all about you—how you look, your age, things you like to do, etc. Write as many sentences as you can going around and around the circle. Then draw a picture of yourself in the center of the circle.

START → *Answers will vary.*

DRAW YOURSELF.

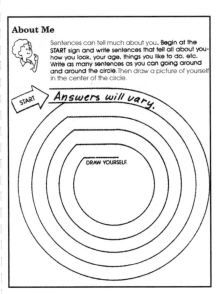

Page 49

A Sensational Scent

Circle the letters that should be capital letters. Then write them in the matching numbered blanks to answer the question.

1. Sadie, Homer's friend, lives on Elm Street.
2. Homer's aunt lives in Kansas City, Kansas.
3. Are you sure Aunt Aggie is coming?
4. Rip Van Winkle came to town.
5. The doughnuts were made by Homer Price.
6. Miss Terwilliger and Uncle Ully saved yarn.
7. Homer Price was written by Robert McCloskey.
8. Uncle Ulysses owned a lunch room.
9. The Super – Duper was a comic book hero.
10. Doc Pelly lived in Homer's town.
11. Money was stolen by the robbers.
12. Now you have the answer to the question.

Who is hiding in the suitcase?

A r o m a   t h e   p e t   s k u n k
3 7 4 11 3   6 5 1   10 1 6   9 2 8 12 2

Page 50

Now, How Does That Go?

Write the sentences correctly. Be sure to put capital letters, periods and exclamation marks where they belong.

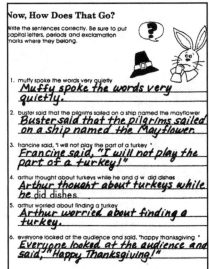

1. muffy spoke the words very quietly
   Muffy spoke the words very quietly.

2. buster said that the pilgrims sailed on a ship named the mayflower
   Buster said that the pilgrims sailed on a ship named the Mayflower.

3. francine said, "i will not play the part of a turkey"
   Francine said, "I will not play the part of a turkey!"

4. arthur thought about turkeys while he and d w did dishes
   Arthur thought about turkeys while he did dishes.

5. arthur worried about finding a turkey
   Arthur worried about finding a turkey.

6. everyone looked at the audience and said, "happy thanksgiving "
   Everyone looked at the audience and said, "Happy Thanksgiving!"

Page 51

Punctuation Magic

POWERFUL PUNCTUATION gives sentences PIZZAZZ!

Write the sentences correctly. Be sure to put capital letters, periods and question marks where they belong.

1. mrs paris talked to richard, alex, matthew and emily about the trip to the museum
Mrs. Paris talked to Richard, Alex, Matthew and Emily about the trip to the museum.

2. the children read a story about a king who was greedy
The children read a story about a king who was greedy.

3. everyone but richard drew a picture about the story
Everyone but Richard drew a picture about the story.

4. why was drake sick
Why was Drake sick?

5. mrs gates asked matthew to take homework to drake
Mrs. Gates asked Matthew to take homework to Drake.

6. did richard's wish make drake sick
Did Richard's wish make Drake sick?

Page 52

An Excellent Exercise

The words **a** and **an** help point out a noun. Use **a** before a word that begins with a consonant. Use **an** before a word that begins with a vowel.

1. Our class visited *a* farm.
2. We could only stay *an* hour.
3. A man let us pick eggs out of *a* nest.
4. We saw *an* egg that was cracked.
5. We watched *a* lady milk a cow.
6. We got to eat *an* ice cream cone.

Page 53

Add an Apostrophe

Add **'s** to a noun to show who or what owns something.

✏ the correct word under each picture.

The ___ nose is big.
clown   clowns   (clown's)

This is ___ coat.
Bettys   (Betty's)   Betty

I know ___ brother.
(Burt's)   Burt   Burts

The ___ hat is pretty.
girls   girl   (girl's)

That is the ___ ball.
(kitten's)   kitten   kittens

My ___ shoe is missing.
sisters   sister   (sister's)

The ___ coach is Mr. Hall.
teams   (team's)   team

The ___ cover is torn.
(book's)   books   book

Page 54

Who Is Hungrier?

Use the pictures to help you complete each sentence with the correct word.

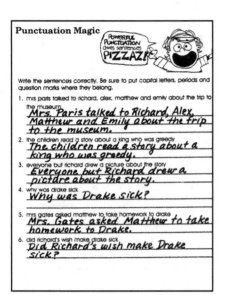

Sludge   Fang   Big Hex

sleepy
sleepier
sleepiest

1. Fang is *sleepier* than Big Hex.
2. Big Hex is *sleepy*.
3. Sludge is the *sleepiest* of all.

Rosamond   Annie   Eric

dirty
dirtier
dirtiest

1. Rosamond's shirt is the *dirtiest* of all.
2. Eric's shirt is *dirtier* than Annie's.
3. Annie's shirt is *dirty*.

Marshmallow   cotton ball   pillow

soft
softer
softest

1. The pillow is *soft*.
2. The cotton ball is the *softest* of all.
3. The marshmallow is *softer* than the pillow.

Nate   Finley   Pip

hungry
hungrier
hungriest

1. Pip is *hungrier* than Nate.
2. Nate is *hungry*.
3. Finley is the *hungriest* of all.

Page 55

Is It a World Record?

Read each sentence. Choose the correct word and write it on the line.

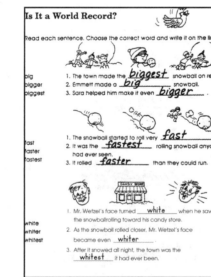

big
bigger
biggest

1. The town made the *biggest* snowball on record.
2. Emmett made a *big* snowball.
3. Sara helped him make it even *bigger*.

fast
faster
fastest

1. The snowball started to roll very *fast*.
2. It was the *fastest* rolling snowball anyone had ever seen.
3. It rolled *faster* than they could run.

white
whiter
whitest

1. Mr. Wetzel's face turned *white* when he saw the snowball rolling toward his candy store.
2. As the snowball rolled closer, Mr. Wetzel's face became even *whiter*.
3. After it snowed all night, the town was the *whitest* it had ever been.

Page 56

Bunny Bunch

There are ten bunnies in this family. Each one is special. Read the clues and fill in the blank with the word that rhymes and makes sense.

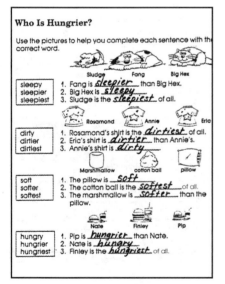

1. I like to hop and drink *pop*
2. I can run fast, but still I am always *last*
3. I like to run and jump, but sometimes I fall and get a *bump*
4. I like to help Mom and Pop by scrubbing the floor with a *mop*
5. After I feed the cat, I take out my baseball and *bat*
6. I like to go on a hike or ride my *bike*
7. I like to dig in the sand and play the drums in a *band*
8. I like to play with a toy car while I eat a candy *bar*
9. I can walk in the fog and also chop a *log*
10. I can fly my kite but not during the *night*

band
bar
bat
bike
bump
cast
daylight
far
fat
fog
hand
last
like
log
mop
night
pop
pump
stop
top

Page 57

Loosey Goosey

Find the names of the birds at the bottom of the page that will rhyme with the words given. For example: Loose goose

narrow *sparrow*
hairy *canary*
men *wren*
pork *stork*
love *dove*
pleasant *pheasant*
perky *turkey*
soon *loon*
luck *duck*
darling *starling*

bobbin *robin*
dark *lark*
pinch *finch*
muffin *puffin*
beagle *eagle*
frail *quail*
hull *gull*
lay *jay*
howl *owl*

dove
stork
canary
wren
robin
jay

starling
sparrow
pheasant
eagle
turkey
owl
gull

quail
loon
puffin
duck
lark
finch

Page 58

Do You Know a Boa?

Print a rhyming word under each word on the boa's body. Slither down from the head to the tail.

words will vary.

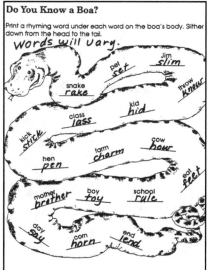

pet *set*
Jim *slim*
throw *know*
snake *rake*
kid *hid*
class *lass*
kick *stick*
cow *how*
farm *charm*
hen *pen*
eat *feet*
mother *brother*
boy *toy*
school *rule*
day *say*
corn *horn*
lend *end*

Page 59

High-Flying Acts

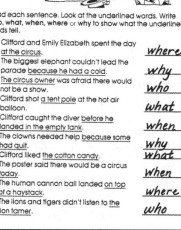

Read each sentence. Look at the underlined words. Write who, what, when, where or why to show what the underlined words tell.

1. Clifford and Emily Elizabeth spent the day <u>at the circus.</u> — *where.*
2. The biggest elephant couldn't lead the parade <u>because he had a cold.</u> — *why*
3. <u>The circus owner</u> was afraid there would not be a show. — *who*
4. Clifford shot <u>a tent pole</u> at the hot air balloon. — *what*
5. Clifford caught the diver <u>before he landed in the empty tank.</u> — *when*
6. The clowns needed help <u>because some had quit.</u> — *why*
7. Clifford liked <u>the cotton candy.</u> — *what*
8. The poster said there would be a circus <u>today.</u> — *When*
9. The human cannon ball landed <u>on top of a haystack.</u> — *where*
10. The lions and tigers didn't listen to the <u>lion tamer.</u> — *who*

Page 60

Donuts, Anyone?

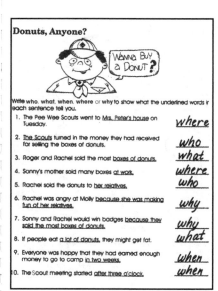

Write who, what, when, where or why to show what the underlined words in each sentence tell you.

1. The Pee Wee Scouts went to <u>Mrs. Peter's house</u> on Tuesday. — *where*
2. <u>The Scouts</u> turned in the money they had received for selling the boxes of donuts. — *who*
3. Roger and Rachel sold the most <u>boxes of donuts.</u> — *what*
4. Sonny's mother sold many boxes <u>at work.</u> — *where*
5. Rachel sold the donuts to <u>her relatives.</u> — *who*
6. Rachel was angry at Molly <u>because she was making fun of her relatives.</u> — *why*
7. Sonny and Rachel would win badges <u>because they sold the most boxes of donuts.</u> — *why*
8. If people eat <u>a lot of donuts,</u> they might get fat. — *what*
9. Everyone was happy that they had earned enough money to go to camp <u>in two weeks.</u> — *when*
10. The Scout meeting started <u>after three o'clock.</u> — *when*

Page 61

It's a Surprise!

Read the clues. Find the answers in the Word Bank.

1. You need snow to do this. You can go fast or slow. You can turn corners. You need a pair of something to do this. What is it? *skiing*

2. This can be soft or hard. It can be made of paper or metal. You need it when you want to buy something. What is it? *money*

3. It is a place where you can buy sweet treats to eat. Many of the treats that can be bought there have to be baked in an oven. What is it? *bakery*

4. In larger cities these come out every day. It can have a few pages or many pages. It tells you what is happening in the world. What is it? *newspaper*

5. It can be large or small. It smells very good. It is green. People like to decorate it at one time of the year. What is it? *Christmas tree.*

6. It needs gas. It is very big. Its driver stops a lot at people's houses to pick up things. What is it? *garbage truck*

Word Bank

book
coins
money
skiing

magazine
paper bag
gas station
sledding

newspaper
holly plant
candy store
bakery

garbage truck
Christmas tree
snowballing

Page 62

Reflect on the Riddles

Read each riddle. Find the answer in the Word Bank and write it on the line.

1. There are two of me. We can blink. We can see. We can wink. We can weep. What are we? *eyes*

2. There is one of me. I can sing. I can form words. I can eat. I can even blow a big bubble. It is green. People eat ice cream, too. What am I? *mouth*

3. There is one of me. If I tickle, I will sneeze. I like to sniff flowers. I like the whiff of hot dogs, also. What am I? *nose*

4. We need to bend and stretch. We need rest. We need to work and we need to play. We are all different. What are we? *bodies*

5. I can be almost any color. I can be long or short. I can be curled and I can be spiked. What am I? *hair*

6. We can change. We can be happy or sad. We can be worried or excited. We can even be scared. What are we? *feelings*

7. I cover a lot. I keep muscles, bones, and blood inside your body. I let you know if it is hot or cold. I tell you if something is wet or dry. What am I? *skin*

8. We all have feelings. We all have bodies. We all like to do many of the same things. But, we also are all very different. Who are we? *people*

Word Bank

bodies eyes
people feelings
hair mouth
nose skin

Page 63

The Adventure Begins

One rainy Saturday morning, Patrick, Brenda, and Jamie decided they needed something new and exciting to do that morning. They took out the telephone book and turned to the yellow pages. In it they found these advertisements for special places to visit.

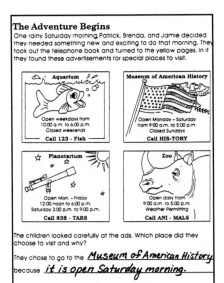

The children looked carefully at the ads. Which place did they choose to visit and why?

They chose to go to the _Museum of American History_
because _it is open Saturday morning._

Page 64

It's a Fact!

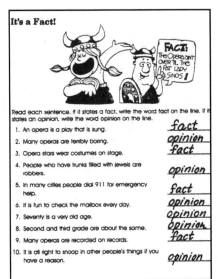

Read each sentence. If it states a fact, write the word fact on the line. If it states an opinion, write the word opinion on the line.

1. An opera is a play that is sung. — _fact_
2. Many operas are terribly boring. — _opinion_
3. Opera stars wear costumes on stage. — _fact_
4. People who have trunks filled with jewels are robbers. — _opinion_
5. In many cities people dial 911 for emergency help. — _fact_
6. It is fun to check the mailbox every day. — _opinion_
7. Seventy is a very old age. — _opinion_
8. Second and third grade are about the same. — _opinion_
9. Many operas are recorded on records. — _fact_
10. It is all right to snoop in other people's things if you have a reason. — _opinion_

Page 65

Is This for Real?

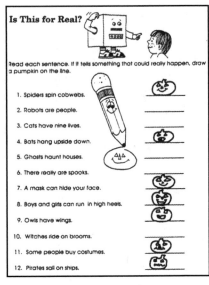

Read each sentence. If it tells something that could really happen, draw a pumpkin on the line.

1. Spiders spin cobwebs.
2. Robots are people.
3. Cats have nine lives.
4. Bats hang upside down.
5. Ghosts haunt houses.
6. There really are spooks.
7. A mask can hide your face.
8. Boys and girls can run in high heels.
9. Owls have wings.
10. Witches ride on brooms.
11. Some people buy costumes.
12. Pirates sail on ships.

Page 66

Top or Bottom?

Read and follow the directions.

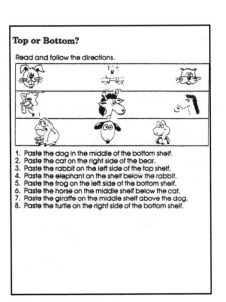

1. Paste the dog in the middle of the bottom shelf.
2. Paste the cat on the right side of the bear.
3. Paste the rabbit on the left side of the top shelf.
4. Paste the elephant on the shelf below the rabbit.
5. Paste the frog on the left side of the bottom shelf.
6. Paste the horse on the middle shelf below the cat.
7. Paste the giraffe on the middle shelf above the dog.
8. Paste the turtle on the right side of the bottom shelf.

Page 67

Where Is It?

Follow the directions. **Hint:** Read through all of the directions before starting.

Pictures will vary.

1. Draw a brown mound in the middle of the box.
2. Draw a red car on top of the mound.
3. Draw apartments behind and to the left of the mound.
4. Draw a bird nest, with four blue eggs inside, on top of the car.
5. Draw three yellow birds flying away from the nest.
6. Draw two tin cans at the bottom of the mound.
7. Put an X on one of the tin cans.
8. Draw you and your friend looking at the car.

Page 69

I'll Try Another Way

Help the little mole find his way to Percy's hut. Read and follow the directions. Write each word that tells what blocks his path as he looks for the loose floorboard. Then draw a line to show where the mole traveled.

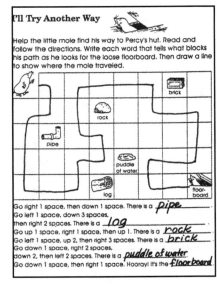

Go right 1 space, then down 1 space. There is a _pipe_
Go left 1 space, down 3 spaces, then right 2 spaces. There is a _log_
Go up 1 space, right 1 space, then up 1. There is a _rock_
Go left 1 space, up 2, then right 3 spaces. There is a _brick_
Go down 1 space, right 2 spaces, down 2, then left 2 spaces. There is a _puddle of water._
Go down 1 space, then right 1 space. Hooray! It's the _floorboard_

Page 70

Build a Community

Cut out the pictures at the bottom of this page. Read the directions. Paste the pictures where they belong.

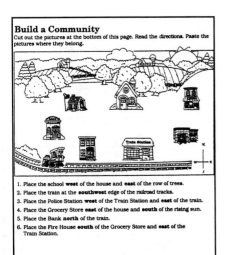

1. Place the school **west** of the house and **east** of the row of trees.
2. Place the train at the **southwest** edge of the railroad tracks.
3. Place the Police Station **west** of the Train Station and **east** of the train.
4. Place the Grocery Store **east** of the house and **south** of the rising sun.
5. Place the Bank **north** of the train.
6. Place the Fire House **south** of the Grocery Store and **east** of the Train Station.

Page 71

Just Being Neighborly

Go along with Percival Porcupine as he delivers the Welcome basket.

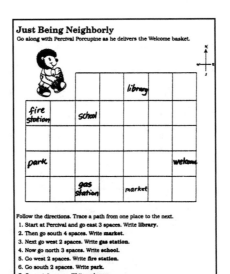

Follow the directions. Trace a path from one place to the next.
1. Start at Percival and go east 3 spaces. Write **library**.
2. Then go south 4 spaces. Write **market**.
3. Next go west 2 spaces. Write **gas station**.
4. Now go north 3 spaces. Write **school**.
5. Go west 2 spaces. Write **fire station**.
6. Go south 2 spaces. Write **park**.
7. Go east 5 spaces. Write **welcome**.

Page 73

Plotting Plants

Follow Rupert Rabbit as he learns about plants. Use the words in the Word Bank to help you.

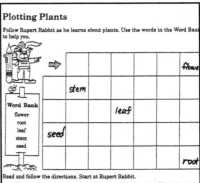

Word Bank: flower, root, leaf, stem, seed

Read and follow the directions. Start at Rupert Rabbit.
1. Go right 5 spaces. Then go down 3 spaces and left 5 spaces. Write the word that names what grows into a new plant here.
2. Now go up 2 spaces. Then go right 6 spaces and down 3 spaces. Write the word that names the part of the plant that is underground here.
3. Now go up 3 spaces. Then go left 3 spaces and down 1 space. Write the word that names the part of the plant that makes the food here.
4. Now go right 2 spaces. Then go up 1 space and left 4 spaces. Write the word that names the part of the plant that carries food and water to the rest of the plant here.
5. Now go down 2 spaces. Then go right 5 spaces and up 3 spaces. Write the word that names the part of the plant that makes the seeds here.

Page 74

What Did I Say?

Unscramble the words in each ⬭. ✏ each sentence on the line.

I'm hiking in the woods.

Today is my friend's birthday.

I will solve this mystery.

The bee stung my finger.

I enjoy being a nurse.

Page 75

The One in the Middle

Print the words in order to make a sentence. The word in the middle is there to help you. Print the sentences.

1. good Dissel jumper Freddy a
Freddy Dissel was _a good jumper._
2. was Gumber teacher Ms.
Ms. Gumber was Freddy's _teacher._
3. and one sister had Freddy one
Freddy had one brother _and one sister._
4. Freddy play going in was to a
Freddy was going to be _in a play._
5. green They face on painted his
They painted green dots _on his face._
6. break Gumber to a told leg Ms.
Ms. Gumber told Freddy _to break a leg._

Now color this picture.

Page 76

What Do I Do First?

Look at the pictures. Number them in the correct order. Then read and number the sentences in the correct order.

3 Cut along the line.
1 Fold a piece of paper in half.
2 Draw one half of a heart on the paper.
4 Open the heart.

3 Draw two antenna on the first heart.
2 Paste the hearts in a line.
4 Then draw two eyes and a mouth on the first heart.
1 Cut out seven small hearts.
What did you make? _caterpillar_

4 Draw two eyes and a nose. Paste a cotton ball on the big heart.
1 Paste a big heart upside down on a piece of paper.
2 Glue a smaller heart upside down on top of the big heart.
3 Paste two long skinny hearts upside down on the smaller heart.
What did you make? _rabbit_

Page 77

Terrific Toast

Lionel said he made the best toast in the world! Number the sentences to show the best order to make terrific toast. The first two are done. *Order may vary.*

13 Close the jar of jam.
6 Close the package of bread.
5 Push down on the toaster button.
11 Put butter on the hot toast.
14 Place the plate of toast on the table and enjoy.
2 Open the package of bread.
1 Plug in the toaster.
10 Put the toast on a plate.
3 Take out two slices of bread.
4 Place the two slices of bread in the toaster.
7 Open the jar of jam.
8 Wait for the toast to pop up.
12 Put jam on the toast.
9 Take the toast out of the toaster.

What do you like to put on your toast? _____

What is your favorite flavor of jam? _____

Page 78

What's What?

Write the words from the Word Bank in the correct category.

Living	Non-Living
1. hen	1. car
2. bird	2. nest
3. kitten	3. boat
4. cow	4. rocks
5. dog	5. plane
6. tree	6. truck

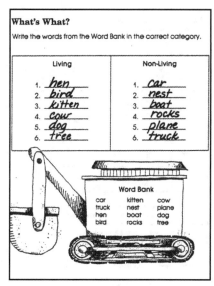

Word Bank

car   kitten   cow
truck   nest   plane
hen   boat   dog
bird   rocks   tree

Page 79

Tidying Up

Write the words from the Word Bank in the correct category.

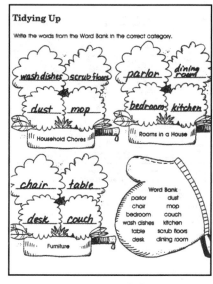

wash dishes   scrub floors   parlor   dining room
dust   mop   bedroom   kitchen

Household Chores   Rooms in a House

chair   table

desk   couch

Word Bank
parlor   dust
chair   mop
bedroom   couch
wash dishes   kitchen
table   scrub floors
desk   dining room

Furniture

Page 80

Cookie Jar

Read the categories on the jars. Cut and paste the cookies in the correct jar.

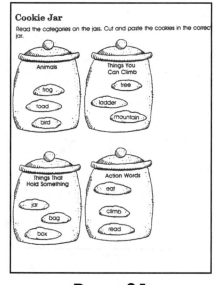

Animals
frog
toad
bird

Things You Can Climb
tree
ladder
mountain

Things That Hold Something
jar
bag
box

Action Words
eat
climb
read

Page 81

Sense-ational!

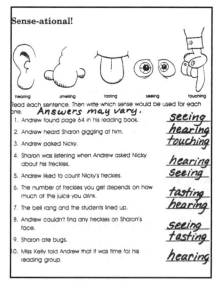

hearing   smelling   tasting   seeing   touching

Read each sentence. Then write which sense would be used for each one. *Answers may vary.*

1. Andrew found page 64 in his reading book.   seeing
2. Andrew heard Sharon giggling at him.   hearing
3. Andrew poked Nicky.   touching
4. Sharon was listening when Andrew asked Nicky about his freckles.   hearing
5. Andrew liked to count Nicky's freckles.   seeing
6. The number of freckles you get depends on how much of the juice you drink.   tasting
7. The bell rang and the students lined up.   hearing
8. Andrew couldn't find any freckles on Sharon's face.   seeing
9. Sharon ate bugs.   tasting
10. Miss Kelly told Andrew that it was time for his reading group.   hearing

Page 83

What's Going On?

Look at the pictures. Find the sentence in the Word Bank that explains each one. Write it on the lines.

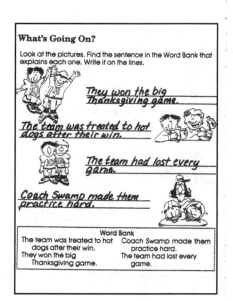

They won the big Thanksgiving game.

The team was treated to hot dogs after their win.

The team had lost every game.

Coach Swamp made them practice hard.

Word Bank
The team was treated to hot dogs after their win.   Coach Swamp made them practice hard.
They won the big Thanksgiving game.   The team had lost every game.

Page 84

Lacy Patterns

Kim likes to look at the lacy patterns of snowflakes with her magnifying glass. Most of them have six sides or six points. But she has never seen two snowflakes that are alike. Kim catches them on small pieces of dark paper so that she can see them better. Some of the snowflakes are broken because they bump into each other as they fall from the clouds.

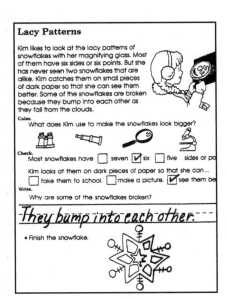

Color.
What does Kim use to make the snowflakes look bigger?

Check.
Most snowflakes have ☐ seven ☑ six ☐ five sides or po

Kim looks at them on dark pieces of paper so that she can...
☐ take them to school. ☐ make a picture. ☑ see them be

Write.
Why are some of the snowflakes broken?

They bump into each other.

• Finish the snowflake.

Page 85

Faraway and Close Up

Kim's favorite subject is science. She has a telescope and a microscope in her bedroom. At night, she looks through her telescope. Things that are far away, like the moon, stars and planets, look bigger. When she looks through her microscope, she can see tiny things close up, like a drop of water or a bit of salt.

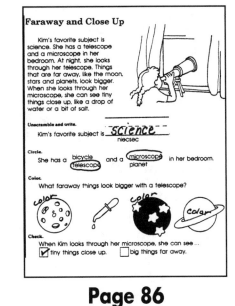

Unscramble and write.
Kim's favorite subject is _science_
niecsec

Circle.
She has a (bicycle) (telescope) and a (microscope) planet in her bedroom.

Color.
What faraway things look bigger with a telescope?

color   color
color

Check.
When Kim looks through her microscope, she can see ...
☑ tiny things close up. ☐ big things far away.

Page 86

Planets

There are eight planets that move around the sun. Our planet is Earth. Earth is closest to Mars and Venus. Jupiter is the largest planet. It is many times larger than Earth. Saturn is the planet with seven rings around it. The smallest planet is called Mercury!

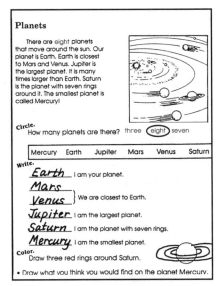

Circle.
How many planets are there? three (eight) seven

| Mercury | Earth | Jupiter | Mars | Venus | Saturn |

Write.
Earth I am your planet.
Mars
Venus } We are closest to Earth.
Jupiter I am the largest planet.
Saturn I am the planet with seven rings.
Mercury I am the smallest planet.

Color.
Draw three red rings around Saturn.

• Draw what you think you would find on the planet Mercury.

Page 87

The Subway

Some big cities have a subway. A subway is a railroad that is under the ground. The trains carry people from one part of the city to another. The trains stop often to let people off and on. Many people ride to work on a subway. Others ride to school or to go shopping. Subways are nice because they do not take up space in a city.

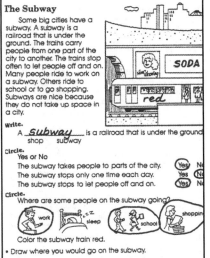

Write.
A _subway_ is a railroad that is under the ground.
shop   subway

Circle.
Yes or No
The subway takes people to parts of the city. (Yes) No
The subway stops only one time each day. Yes (No)
The subway stops to let people off and on. (Yes) No

Circle.
Where are some people on the subway going?

work   sleep   school   shopping

Color the subway train red.

• Draw where you would go on the subway.

Page 88

A Helicopter

Would you like to ride in a helicopter? A helicopter flies in the air. It can fly up and down. It can fly forward and backward. It can fly sideways. A helicopter can even stay in one spot in the air! Helicopters can be many sizes. Some helicopters carry just one person. Some carry 30 people. Helicopters can be used for many jobs.

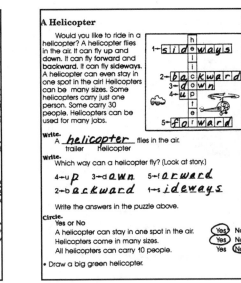

1- s i d e w a y s
2- b a c k w a r d
3- d o w n
4- u p
5- f o r w a r d

Write.
A _helicopter_ flies in the air.
trailer   Helicopter

Write.
Which way can a helicopter fly? (Look at story.)

4-u p   3-d o w n   5-f o r w a r d
2-b a c k w a r d   1-s i d e w a y s

Write the answers in the puzzle above.

Circle.
Yes or No
A helicopter can stay in one spot in the air. (Yes) No
Helicopters come in many sizes. (Yes) No
All helicopters can carry 10 people. Yes (No)

• Draw a big green helicopter.

Page 89

Hot Air Balloons

Would you like to fly in a hot air balloon? A hot air balloon can fly when it is filled with hot air or a gas, called helium. Most hot air balloons use helium to fly. People can ride in a basket that is tied to the balloon. The wind moves the balloon in the sky. To come down, the people must let some of the air or gas out of the balloon.

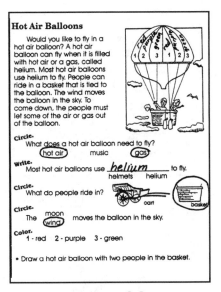

Circle.
What does a hot air balloon need to fly?
(hot air)   music   (gas)

Write.
Most hot air balloons use _helium_ to fly.
helmets   helium

Circle.
What do people ride in?   cart   basket

Circle.
The (moon) (wind) moves the balloon in the sky.

Color.
1 - red   2 - purple   3 - green

• Draw a hot air balloon with two people in the basket.

Page 90

What an Act!

Read about each act. Read the titles in the Word Bank. Write the best title for each act.

1. The lady climbed on the horse's back. The horse galloped around the ring as she stood up on its back.
Lady on a Galloping Horse

2. Four seals stood up on their flippers. They spun and tossed a ball to each other. The biggest seal threw it to his trainer, Mac, who threw it back.
Mac and His Ball-Playing Seals

3. The trainer led the five bears into the ring. Each bear had its own bike. They rode up and down ramps as they raced each other around the ring.
The Bike-Riding Bears

4. The clowns tumbled as they came into the ring. They did forward rolls, backward rolls and even walked on their hands.
The Tumbling Clowns

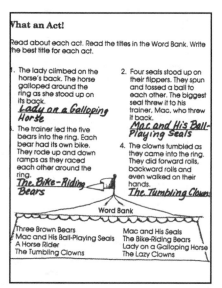

Word Bank

Three Brown Bears
Mac and His Ball-Playing Seals
A Horse Rider
The Tumbling Clowns

Mac and His Seals
The Bike-Riding Bears
Lady on a Galloping Horse
The Lazy Clowns

Page 91

Can I, or Can't I?

Read each sentence. Write **can** or **can't** on the line.

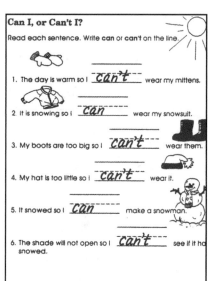

1. The day is warm so I _can't_ wear my mittens.

2. It is snowing so I _can_ wear my snowsuit.

3. My boots are too big so I _can't_ wear them.

4. My hat is too little so I _can't_ wear it.

5. It snowed so I _can_ make a snowman.

6. The shade will not open so I _can't_ see if it has snowed.

Page 92

Just Rolling Along!

Help Emmett roll the snowball down the hill. Read the clues. Then find the words in the Word Bank and write them in the correct spaces. Hint: The last letter of each answer is the first letter of the next answer.

1. Boasting
2. Very, very good
3. Many moving cars and trucks
4. A little cold
5. Paid attention
6. Twice an amount
7. Comes after seventh
8. One of two equal parts
9. Very well-known
10. Not crooked

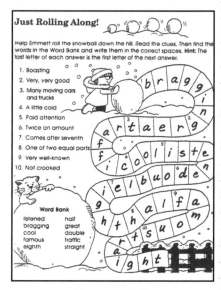

Word Bank

listened   half
bragging   great
cool   double
famous   traffic
eighth   straight

Page 93

A-maze-ing

Draw a line through the maze in the order of the clues to help baby bird find his way back to his nest.

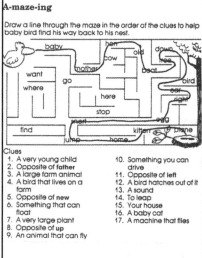

Clues

1. A very young child
2. Opposite of father
3. A large farm animal
4. A bird that lives on a farm
5. Opposite of new
6. Something that can float
7. A very large plant
8. Opposite of up
9. An animal that can fly
10. Something you can drive
11. Opposite of left
12. A bird hatches out of it
13. A sound
14. To leap
15. Your house
16. A baby cat
17. A machine that flies

Page 94

Circus Sights

Find the answers to the puzzle in the Word Bank.

Across
1. To save from danger
4. The last act
6. A silly person
8. Your mistake
10. To give an order
11. A poster

Down
2. A large weapon
3. A show with clowns and animal acts
5. You dress up in these
7. Great
9. A person who trains animals
11. A trick

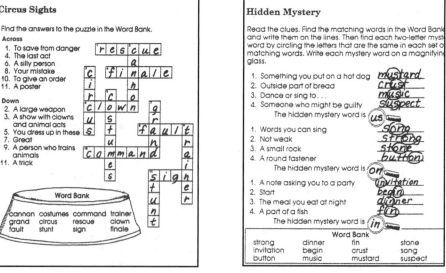

Word Bank

cannon   costumes   command   trainer
grand   circus   rescue   clown
fault   stunt   sign   finale

Page 95

Hidden Mystery

Read the clues. Find the matching words in the Word Bank and write them on the lines. Then find each two-letter mystery word by circling the letters that are the same in each set of matching words. Write each mystery word on a magnifying glass.

1. Something you put on a hot dog — mustard
2. Outside part of bread — crust
3. Dance or sing to . . . — music
4. Someone who might be guilty — suspect
   The hidden mystery word is — us

1. Words you can sing — song
2. Not weak — strong
3. A small rock — stone
4. A round fastener — button
   The hidden mystery word is — on

1. A note asking you to a party — invitation
2. Start — begin
3. The meal you eat at night — dinner
4. A part of a fish — fin
   The hidden mystery word is — in

Word Bank

strong   dinner   fin   stone
invitation   begin   crust   song
button   music   mustard   suspect

Page 96

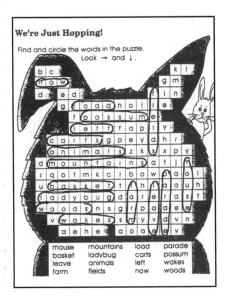

We're Just Hopping!

Find and circle the words in the puzzle.
Look → and ↓.

mouse	mountains	load	parade
basket	ladybug	carts	possum
leave	animals	left	wakes
farm	fields	now	woods

Page 97

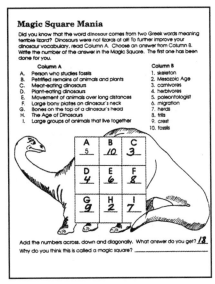

Magic Square Mania

Did you know that the word dinosaur comes from two Greek words meaning terrible lizard? Dinosaurs were not lizards at all! To further improve your dinosaur vocabulary, read Column A. Choose an answer from Column B. Write the number of the answer in the Magic Square. The first one has been done for you.

Column A
A. Person who studies fossils
B. Petrified remains of animals and plants
C. Meat-eating dinosaurs
D. Plant-eating dinosaurs
E. Movement of animals over long distances
F. Large bony plates on dinosaur's neck
G. Bones on the top of a dinosaur's head
H. The Age of Dinosaurs
I. Large groups of animals that live together

Column B
1. skeleton
2. Mesozoic Age
3. carnivores
4. herbivores
5. paleontologist
6. migration
7. herds
8. frills
9. crest
10. fossils

A 5	B 10	C 3
D 4	E 6	F 8
G 9	H 2	I 7

Add the numbers across, down and diagonally. What answer do you get? _18_
Why do you think this is called a magic square? _____

Page 98

Body Works

Read the clues. Write the words in the puzzle.

Across:
2. You use these to breathe.
4. You need to do this when you're tired.
5. This breaks down food.
7. This tells your body what to do.
9. A gas you breathe.
10. It pumps blood.

Down:
1. It carries oxygen to your body.
3. Microscopic living things that can make you sick.
6. This helps when you are sick.
8. These support and shape your body.

bones rest
germs
brain lungs
heart oxygen medicine
        blood
        stomach

b l u n g s
o   r e s t
o   m
d   s t o m a c
    d
    b r a i n
    c
    i
    b o x y g e n
    n
    h e a r t

Page 99

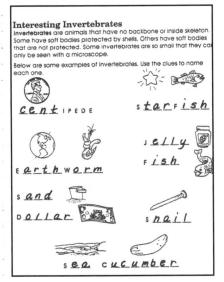

Interesting Invertebrates

Invertebrates are animals that have no backbone or inside skeleton. Some have soft bodies protected by shells. Others have soft bodies that are not protected. Some invertebrates are so small that they can only be seen with a microscope.

Below are some examples of invertebrates. Use the clues to name each one.

c e n t IPEDE

s t a r f i s h

j e l l y
f i s h

E a r t h w o r m

s a n d

D o l l a r

s n a i l

s e a c u c u m b e r

Page 100

Fine, Feathered Friends

Do the puzzle about birds.
Color only the birds.

f
w a r m
e
eggs
t
h
b e
i r
l
l u n g s

Down
1. _____ keep a bird's body warm and dry.
4. A bird uses its _____ to pick up food.

Across
2. A bird is a _____-blooded animal.
3. Baby birds are hatched from _____.
5. Birds breathe with their _____.

| Word Bank | | | | |
| feathers | bill | lungs | eggs | warm |

Page 101

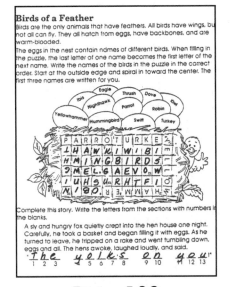

Birds of a Feather

Birds are the only animals that have feathers. All birds have wings, but not all can fly. They all hatch from eggs, have backbones, and are warm-blooded.

The eggs in the nest contain names of different birds. When filling in the puzzle, the last letter of one name becomes the first letter of the next name. Write the names of the birds in the puzzle in the correct order. Start at the outside edge and spiral in toward the center. The first three names are written for you.

Ibis Eagle Thrush Dove Kiwi
Nighthawk Parrot Robin
Yellowhammer Hummingbird Swift Turkey

P A R R O T U R K E
L H A W K I W I B I
H M I N G B I R D S
9 M E L G A E V O W
I U H S U R H T F I
N O B I N A M E R R

Complete this story. Write the letters from the sections with numbers in the blanks.

A sly and hungry fox quietly crept into the hen house one night. Carefully, he took a basket and began filling it with eggs. As he turned to leave, he tripped on a rake and went tumbling down, eggs and all. The hens awoke, laughed loudly, and said,
"_The_ _yolks_ _on_ _you_!"
 1 2 3 4 5 6 7 8 9 10 11 12 13

Page 102

A Mixture of Mammals

Mammals live in many different places. They are a special group because they . . .

- can give milk to their babies.
- protect and guide their young.
- are warm-blooded.
- have hair at some time during their lives.
- have a large, well-developed brain.

Below are some silly pictures made from two mammals put together. Write the names of the two real mammals on the lines. The last letter(s) in the name of the first animal is the first letter(s) in the name of the second animal. The first one is done for you.

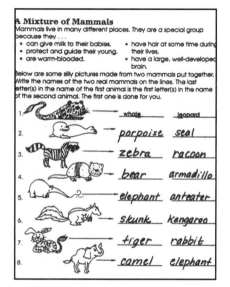

1. whale — leopard
2. porpoise — seal
3. zebra — racoon
4. bear — armadillo
5. elephant — anteater
6. skunk — kangaroo
7. tiger — rabbit
8. camel — elephant

Page 103

Dynamic Dinosaurs

Dinosaurs were reptiles that lived millions of years ago. Some of them were the biggest animals to ever live on land. Some were as small as chickens. Some dinosaurs ate plants, while other were meat-eaters.

Scientists have given names to the dinosaurs that often describe their special bodies, sizes, and habits.

Look at the object(s) placed in the picture with each dinosaur. Use the objects as clues to fill in the blanks and finish each dinosaur's name.

TRICERA **TOPS**

LAMB EOSAURUS

DIME TRODON

SALT ASAURUS

PLATE OSAURUS

Page 104

Dial a Dinosaur

Danny loves dinosaurs. In fact, he loves them so much that everyone calls him Dinosaur Danny! Find out what Dinosaur Danny's favorite dinosaur is by decoding the message below. To do this, use the numbers on the telephone and the directional markers.

For example: 3 points to the letter D.

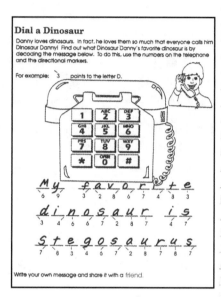

My favorite
dinosaur is
Stegosaurus

Write your own message and share it with a friend.

Page 105

Hawaii

Fill in the crossword puzzle. The Word Box will help you

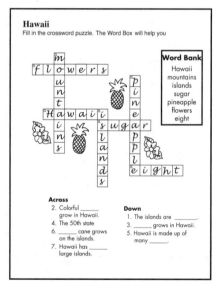

Word Bank
Hawaii
mountains
islands
sugar
pineapple
flowers
eight

Across
2. Colorful _____ grow in Hawaii.
4. The 50th state
6. _____ cane grows on the islands.
7. Hawaii has large islands.

Down
1. The islands are _____.
3. _____ grows in Hawaii.
5. Hawaii is made up of many _____.

Page 106

Follow That Sign!

Look at the road sign symbols below. Each sign is matched to a letter. Use the road sign code to find the names of four vehicles that travel on roads.

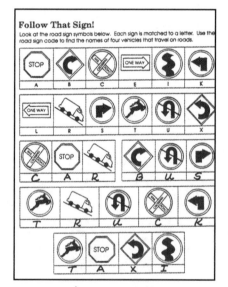

CAR
BUS
TRUCK
TAXI

Page 107

From the Inside Out

Animals whose skeletons have backbones are called **vertebrates**. The backbone, or spine, is made up of bones called **vertebrae**.

Look at the skeletons below. Use the riddle and the Word Bank to write the name of each vertebrate.

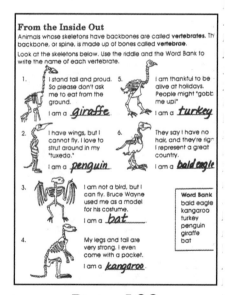

1. I stand tall and proud. So please don't ask me to eat from the ground.
   I am a **giraffe**.

2. I have wings, but I cannot fly. I love to strut around in my "tuxedo."
   I am a **penguin**.

3. I am not a bird, but I can fly. Bruce Wayne used me as a model for his costume.
   I am a **bat**.

4. My legs and tail are very strong. I even come with a pocket.
   I am a **kangaroo**.

5. I am thankful to be alive at holidays. People might "gobble" me up!
   I am a **turkey**.

6. They say I have no hair, and they're right. I represent a great country.
   I am a **bald eagle**.

Word Bank
bald eagle
kangaroo
turkey
penguin
giraffe
bat

Page 108

Whose House?

Use the pictures of the Native American houses to answer the riddles.

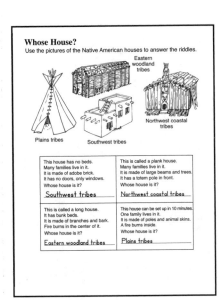

This house has no beds.
Many families live in it.
It is made of adobe brick.
It has no doors, only windows.
Whose house is it?
Southwest tribes

This is called a plank house.
Many families live in it.
It is made of large beams and trees.
It has a totem pole in front.
Whose house is it?
Northwest coastal tribes

This is called a long house.
It has bunk beds.
It is made of branches and bark.
Fire burns in the center of it.
Whose house is it?
Eastern woodland tribes

This house can be set up in 10 minutes.
One family lives in it.
It is made of poles and animal skins.
A fire burns inside.
Whose house is it?
Plains tribes

Page 109

A Family of Friends

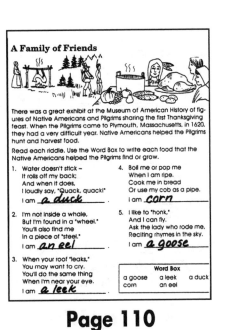

There was a great exhibit at the Museum of American History of figures of Native Americans and Pilgrims sharing the first Thanksgiving feast. When the Pilgrims came to Plymouth, Massachusetts, in 1620, they had a very difficult year. Native Americans helped the Pilgrims hunt and harvest food.

Read each riddle. Use the Word Box to write each food that the Native Americans helped the Pilgrims find or grow.

1. Water doesn't stick –
   It rolls off my back;
   And when it does,
   I loudly say, "Quack, quack!"
   I am **a duck** .

2. I'm not inside a whale,
   But I'm found in a "wheel."
   You'll also find me
   In a piece of "steel."
   I am **an eel** .

3. When your roof "leaks,"
   You may want to cry.
   You'll do the same thing
   When I'm near your eye.
   I am **a leek** .

4. Boil me or pop me
   When I am ripe.
   Cook me in bread
   Or use my cob as a pipe.
   I am **corn** .

5. I like to "honk,"
   And I can fly.
   Ask the lady who rode me,
   Reciting rhymes in the sky.
   I am **a goose** .

Word Box		
a goose	a leek	a duck
corn	an eel	

Page 110

Landform Riddles

Use the Word Bank to solve the riddles. Then color the pictures.

		Word Bank			
lake	island	plain	river	mountain	peninsula

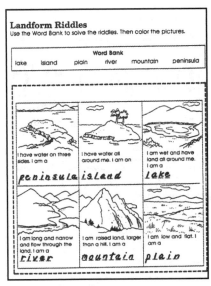

I have water on three sides. I am a **peninsula**

I have water all around me. I am an **island**

I am wet and have land all around me. I am a **lake**

I am long and narrow and flow through the land. I am a **river**

I am raised land, larger than a hill. I am a **mountain**

I am low and flat. I am a **plain**

Page 111

The Reptile House

There are about 6,000 different kinds of reptiles. They come in all sort of shapes and colors. Their sizes in length range from 2 inches to almost 30 feet. Reptiles can be found on every continent except Antarctica. Even though reptiles can seem quite different, they all .

- breathe with lungs.
- are cold-blooded.
- have dry, scaly skin.
- have a backbone.

In the Reptile House at the zoo, each animal needs to be placed in the correct area. Read the information about each reptile. Then use the clues and the pictures to write the name of each reptile in its are

Giant Tortoise can live over 100 years. It can hide under its shell for protection.

Reticulated Python is the longest snake. One was almost 33 feet long.

Saltwater Crocodile is one of the largest reptiles. It can weigh 1,000 lb.

Komodo Dragon is a dragon-like reptile. It is the largest living lizard.

Tuatara is closely related to the extinct dinosaur.

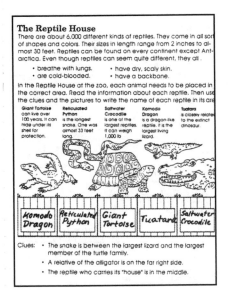

| Komodo Dragon | Reticulated Python | Giant Tortoise | Tuatara | Saltwater Crocodile |

Clues: • The snake is between the largest lizard and the largest member of the turtle family.
• A relative of the alligator is on the far right side.
• The reptile who carries its "house" is in the middle.

Page 112

Pottery Patterns

Before beginning a project, an artist who makes pottery must think about how the piece will be used, what type of clay to use, and what color and patterns to use.

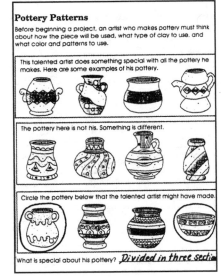

This talented artist does something special with all the pottery he makes. Here are some examples of his pottery.

The pottery here is not his. Something is different.

Circle the pottery below that the talented artist might have made.

What is special about his pottery? **Divided in three secti**

Page 113

Dressing the Part

People who act in plays are called **actors** and **actresses**. For each play, costumes are chosen that make the characters in the story seem more realistic.

Below is the inside of a costume closet.

Pretend that you want to act in some silly plays. Look at the titles of each play below. Write the names of the two costumes you would combine to fit the main character of each play.

1. "The Strong, Flying Ape" **Superman Gorilla**
2. "The Invisible Man on His Horse" **Cowboy Ghost**
3. "The Cat Who Squeaked" **Mouse Lion**
4. "Her Royal Highness Barks up the Wrong Tree" **Princess Dog**
5. "Flying Animal-like Man Saves Building from Fire" **Batman Dragon**

Page 114

Everyone Is Welcome

Cut out the pictures of the people at the bottom of the page. Read the clues carefully. Paste the people where they belong at the table.

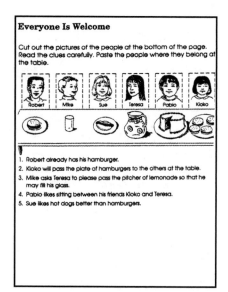

1. Robert already has his hamburger.
2. Kloko will pass the plate of hamburgers to the others at the table.
3. Mike asks Teresa to please pass the pitcher of lemonade so that he may fill his glass.
4. Pablo likes sitting between his friends Kloko and Teresa.
5. Sue likes hot dogs better than hamburgers.

Page 115

Comparing the Seasons

Each of the four seasons (winter, spring, summer, autumn) has certain characteristics. Choose two of the seasons and write their names on the lines above each shape below. Then, complete the other lines with words that describe the season. In the center area, write words that describe both seasons. This is called a **Venn diagram**.

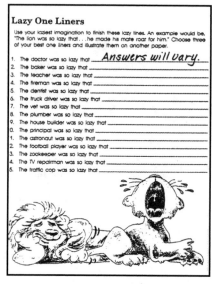

Answers will vary.

Page 117

Lazy One Liners

Use your laziest imagination to finish these lazy lines. An example would be, "The lion was so lazy that . . .he made his mate roar for him." Choose three of your best one liners and illustrate them on another paper.

1. The doctor was so lazy that _____ Answers will vary.
2. The baker was so lazy that _____
3. The teacher was so lazy that _____
4. The fireman was so lazy that _____
5. The dentist was so lazy that _____
6. The truck driver was so lazy that _____
7. The vet was so lazy that _____
8. The plumber was so lazy that _____
9. The house builder was so lazy that _____
10. The principal was so lazy that _____
11. The astronaut was so lazy that _____
12. The football player was so lazy that _____
13. The zookeeper was so lazy that _____
14. The TV repairman was so lazy that _____
15. The traffic cop was so lazy that _____

Page 118

A Story for the People

Look carefully at the picture on the buckskin. Write a story on the lines to tell what is happening in the picture.

Stories will vary.

Page 119

Using Descriptive Language

Stories are always more exciting when you can picture them happening in your mind. Descriptive words help make the story imaginable. Use these categories to think of words that describe a walk along the beach. Pretend you are barefoot walking close to the water. With a partner, write three words in each area. Then, use all the words in a story.

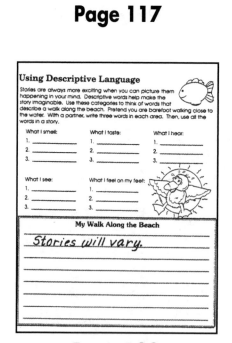

What I smell:
1. _____
2. _____
3. _____

What I taste:
1. _____
2. _____
3. _____

What I hear:
1. _____
2. _____
3. _____

What I see:
1. _____
2. _____
3. _____

What I feel on my feet:
1. _____
2. _____
3. _____

My Walk Along the Beach

Stories will vary.

Page 120

Ready to Mail

Read the envelope Tilly addressed to Mr. Bunny.

tilly mole
102 garden road
forest maine 25136

mr bunny
523 sweet potato lane
forest maine 25136

Address the envelope correctly. Be sure to use capital letters, periods and commas where they belong.

Tilly Mole
102 Garden Road
Forest, Maine, 25136

Mr. Bunny
523 Sweet Potato Lane
Forest, Maine 25136

Draw and color a stamp on the envelope.

Page 121

Write, Please

Read the thank you letter Louis wrote to his Uncle McAllister.

october 5 2014

dear uncle mcallister
        thank you for the tadpole   i named him
alphonse   he likes to eat cheeseburgers   this is the
best gift you ever sent me
            thank you again
                    love
                    louis

Write the letter correctly. Be sure to use capital letters, periods and commas where they belong.

October 5, 2014

Dear Uncle McAllister;
    Thank you for the tadpole. I
named him Alphonse. He likes to
eat cheeseburgers. This is the
best gift you ever sent me.
Thank you again.

            Love,
            Louis

Page 122

Writing Haiku Poetry

Haiku poetry is originally from the country of Japan. It is a very simple form of poetry and does not have to rhyme.

Example	Poem Pattern
The polar bear cubs	5 syllables
learn to swim and dive for fish	7 syllables
in the cold, blue sea.	5 syllables

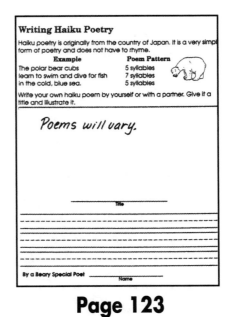

Write your own haiku poem by yourself or with a partner. Give it a title and illustrate it.

Poems will vary.

_____ Title

By a Beary Special Poet _____ Name

Page 123

Just Napping

Count. Write the correct number of cats in the box on each cat bed.

Page 126

Unpack the Teddy Bears

Cut out the bears at the bottom of the page. Paste them where they belong in numbered order.

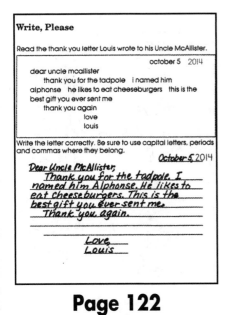

Page 127

Plump Piglets

Pigs like to eat corn. These little pigs just ate lunch.
Read the clues to find out how many ears of corn each pig ate. Write the number on the line below each pig.

Who ate the most and was really piggy? *Portly*
Who ate the least? *Patsy*

Page 129

Two by Two

Finish counting.

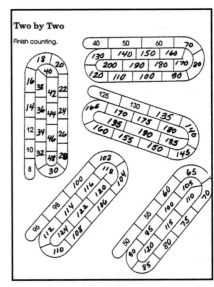

Page 130

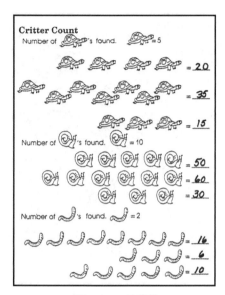

Critter Count

Number of 🐢's found. 🐢🐢 = 5

🐢🐢🐢🐢 = 20

🐢🐢🐢🐢🐢🐢🐢 = 35

🐢🐢🐢 = 15

Number of 🐌's found. 🐌 = 10

🐌🐌🐌🐌🐌 = 50

🐌🐌🐌🐌🐌🐌 = 60

🐌🐌🐌 = 30

Number of 🪱's found. 🪱 = 2

🪱🪱🪱🪱🪱🪱🪱🪱 = 16

🪱🪱🪱 = 6

🪱🪱🪱🪱🪱 = 10

Page 131

Air Bear Addition

Help Buddy off the ground. Solve the problems. Then color the clouds with sums of 9 to find the right path.

Page 132

Math-Minded Mermaids

Each mermaid sits upon her own special rock.

Look at the number on each shell. Then look → and ↓ in the number boxes. Circle each pair of numbers that can be added together to equal the number in the shell the mermaid is holding.

Page 133

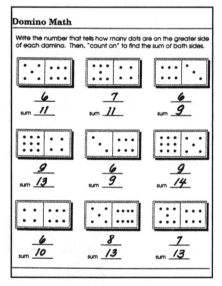

Domino Math

Write the number that tells how many dots are on the greater side of each domino. Then, "count on" to find the sum of both sides.

6 — sum 11

7 — sum 11

6 — sum 9

9 — sum 13

6 — sum 9

9 — sum 14

6 — sum 10

8 — sum 13

7 — sum 13

Page 134

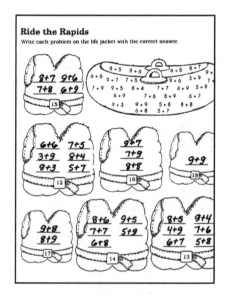

Ride the Rapids

Write each problem on the life jacket with the correct answer.

8+7   9+6
7+8   6+9
— 15

6+6
3+9
9+3
— 12

7+5
8+4
5+7
— 16

9+7
7+9
8+8
— 18

9+9

8+6
7+7
6+8
— 17

9+5
5+9
— 14

8+5
4+9
6+7
— 13

9+4
7+6
5+8

Page 135

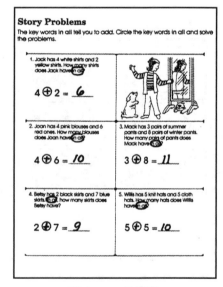

Story Problems

The key words in all tell you to add. Circle the key words in all and solve the problems.

1. Jack has 4 white shirts and 2 yellow shirts. How many shirts does Jack have in all?

4 ⊕ 2 = 6

2. Joan has 4 pink blouses and 6 red ones. How many blouses does Joan have in all?

4 ⊕ 6 = 10

3. Mack has 3 pairs of summer pants and 8 pairs of winter pants. How many pairs of pants does Mack have in all?

3 ⊕ 8 = 11

4. Betsy has 2 black skirts and 7 blue skirts. In all, how many skirts does Betsy have?

2 ⊕ 7 = 9

5. Willis has 5 knit hats and 5 cloth hats. How many hats does Willis have in all?

5 ⊕ 5 = 10

Page 136

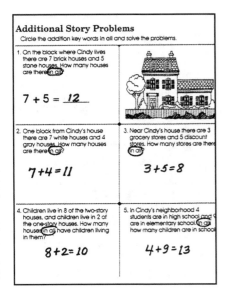

Additional Story Problems
Circle the addition key words in all and solve the problems.

1. On the block where Cindy lives there are 7 brick houses and 5 stone houses. How many houses are there in all?

$7 + 5 = \underline{12}$

2. One block from Cindy's house there are 7 white houses and 4 gray houses. How many houses are there in all?

$7 + 4 = 11$

3. Near Cindy's house there are 3 grocery stores and 5 discount stores. How many stores are there in all?

$3 + 5 = 8$

4. Children live in 8 of the two-story houses, and children live in 2 of the one-story houses. How many houses in all have children living in them?

$8 + 2 = 10$

5. In Cindy's neighborhood 4 students are in high school and 9 are in elementary school. In all how many children are in school?

$4 + 9 = 13$

Page 137

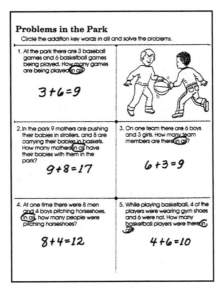

Problems in the Park
Circle the addition key words in all and solve the problems.

1. At the park there are 3 baseball games and 6 basketball games being played. How many games are being played in all?

$3 + 6 = 9$

2. In the park 9 mothers are pushing their babies in strollers, and 8 are carrying their babies in baskets. How many mothers in all have their babies with them in the park?

$9 + 8 = 17$

3. On one team there are 6 boys and 3 girls. How many team members are there in all?

$6 + 3 = 9$

4. At one time there were 8 men and 4 boys pitching horseshoes. In all, how many people were pitching horseshoes?

$8 + 4 = 12$

5. While playing basketball, 4 of the players were wearing gym shoes and 6 were not. How many basketball players were there in all?

$4 + 6 = 10$

Page 138

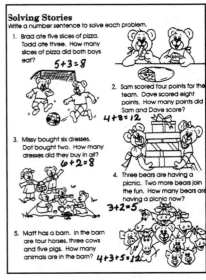

Solving Stories
Write a number sentence to solve each problem.

1. Brad ate five slices of pizza. Todd ate three. How many slices of pizza did both boys eat?

$5 + 3 = 8$

2. Sam scored four points for the team. Dave scored eight points. How many points did Sam and Dave score?

$4 + 8 = 12$

3. Missy bought six dresses. Dot bought two. How many dresses did they buy in all?

$6 + 2 = 8$

4. Three bears are having a picnic. Two more bears join the fun. How many bears are having a picnic now?

$3 + 2 = 5$

5. Matt has a barn. In the barn are four horses, three cows and five pigs. How many animals are in the barn?

$4 + 3 + 5 = 12$

Page 139

Training with Facts
Use the numbers on each train to write the fact families.

8 6 14

$8 + 6 = 14$
$6 + 8 = 14$
$14 - 6 = 8$
$14 - 8 = 6$

6 15 9

$6 + 9 = 15$
$9 + 6 = 15$
$15 - 9 = 6$
$15 - 6 = 9$

17 8 9

$8 + 9 = 17$
$9 + 8 = 17$
$17 - 8 = 9$
$17 - 9 = 8$

9 5 14

$9 + 5 = 14$
$5 + 9 = 14$
$14 - 9 = 5$
$14 - 5 = 9$

Page 140

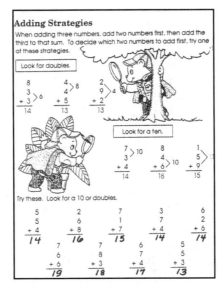

Adding Strategies
When adding three numbers, add two numbers first, then add the third to that sum. To decide which two numbers to add first, try one of these strategies.

Look for doubles.

$\begin{array}{r}8\\3\\+3\\\hline14\end{array}$ $\begin{array}{r}8\\4\\+5\\\hline13\end{array}$ $\begin{array}{r}2\\9\\+2\\\hline13\end{array}$

Look for a ten.

$\begin{array}{r}7\\3\\+4\\\hline14\end{array}$ $\begin{array}{r}8\\4\\+6\\\hline18\end{array}$ $\begin{array}{r}1\\5\\+9\\\hline15\end{array}$

Try these. Look for a 10 or doubles.

$\begin{array}{r}5\\5\\+4\\\hline14\end{array}$ $\begin{array}{r}2\\2\\+8\\\hline16\end{array}$ $\begin{array}{r}7\\7\\+7\\\hline15\end{array}$ $\begin{array}{r}3\\7\\+4\\\hline14\end{array}$ $\begin{array}{r}6\\2\\+6\\\hline14\end{array}$

$\begin{array}{r}7\\6\\+6\\\hline19\end{array}$ $\begin{array}{r}7\\8\\+3\\\hline18\end{array}$ $\begin{array}{r}6\\7\\+4\\\hline17\end{array}$ $\begin{array}{r}5\\5\\+3\\\hline13\end{array}$

Page 141

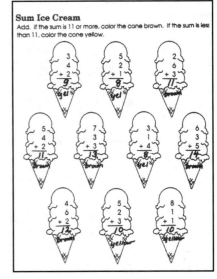

Sum Ice Cream
Add. If the sum is 11 or more, color the cone brown. If the sum is less than 11, color the cone yellow.

$\begin{array}{r}3\\4\\+2\\\hline9\end{array}$ yel $\begin{array}{r}5\\2\\+1\\\hline8\end{array}$ yel $\begin{array}{r}2\\6\\+3\\\hline11\end{array}$ brown

$\begin{array}{r}5\\4\\+2\\\hline11\end{array}$ brown $\begin{array}{r}7\\3\\+3\\\hline13\end{array}$ brown $\begin{array}{r}3\\1\\+4\\\hline8\end{array}$ yel $\begin{array}{r}6\\3\\+5\\\hline14\end{array}$ brown

$\begin{array}{r}4\\6\\+2\\\hline12\end{array}$ brown $\begin{array}{r}5\\2\\+3\\\hline10\end{array}$ yellow $\begin{array}{r}8\\1\\+1\\\hline10\end{array}$ yellow

Page 142

Path Problems

Add. Show the detective the correct path. Color the path with sums of 13.

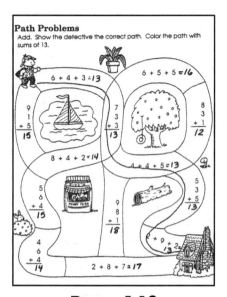

$6 + 4 + 3 = 13$

$6 + 5 + 5 = 16$

$8 + 4 + 2 = 14$

$4 + 4 + 5 = 13$

$2 + 8 + 7 = 17$

$$\begin{array}{r} 9 \\ 1 \\ +5 \\ \hline 15 \end{array} \quad \begin{array}{r} 7 \\ 3 \\ +3 \\ \hline 13 \end{array} \quad \begin{array}{r} 8 \\ 3 \\ +1 \\ \hline 12 \end{array}$$

$$\begin{array}{r} 5 \\ 6 \\ +4 \\ \hline 15 \end{array} \quad \begin{array}{r} 9 \\ 8 \\ +1 \\ \hline 18 \end{array} \quad \begin{array}{r} 5 \\ 3 \\ +5 \\ \hline 13 \end{array}$$

$$\begin{array}{r} 4 \\ 6 \\ +4 \\ \hline 14 \end{array} \quad \begin{array}{r} +9 \\ 13 \end{array}$$

Page 143

Something's Missing

In the forest, 13 animals have a picnic. Skunk brings 8 sandwiches. How many sandwiches should Raccoon bring so that each animal can have one?

$8 + \underline{?} = 13$

What number added to 8 equals 13?
To find the missing addend, find the difference of 13 and 8. That is, subtract the given addend (8) from the sum (13).

$13 - 8 = \underline{5}$

Since $13 - 8 = 5$, then $8 + \underline{5} = 13$.
Raccoon should bring $\underline{5}$ sandwiches.

Try these. Find the missing addends.

$\underline{9} + 6 = 15 \qquad \underline{6} + 7 = 13$

$9 + \underline{5} = 14 \qquad 8 + \underline{6} = 14$

$\underline{8} + 8 = 16 \qquad 9 + \underline{9} = 18$

Page 144

Food Fun

The table below tells what each animal brought to the picnic. Fill in the missing numbers.

Animal	Vegetables	Fruits	Total
Skunk	8	6	14
Raccoon	9	8	17
Squirrel	7	8	15
Rabbit	6	7	13
Owl	7	9	16
Deer	9	9	18

Write the name of the animal that answers each question.

1. Who brought the same number of vegetables as fruits? _deer_
2. Who brought two more fruits than vegetables? _Owl_
3. Who brought two more vegetables than fruits? _skunk_
4. Which two animals brought one more fruit than vegetables? _rabbit_ and _squirrel_
5. Which two animals brought the most vegetables? _deer_ and _racoon_
6. Which two animals brought the most fruit? _deer_ and _owl_
7. Which animal brought the least vegetables? _rabbit_
8. Which animal brought the least fruit? _skunk_
9. Who brought more fruit, Skunk and Squirrel, or Raccoon and Rabbit? _racoon & rabbit_

Page 145

Circus Fun

Add. Remember to add the ones first.

tens	ones
2	5
+1	4
3	**9**

tens	ones
5	3
+3	2
8	**5**

tens	ones
7	1
+2	8
9	**9**

tens	ones
4	4
+3	2
7	**6**

tens	ones
5	1
+2	2
8	**8**

tens	ones
2	6
+5	2
7	**8**

tens	ones
2	6
+4	2
6	**8**

tens	ones
3	7
+5	1
8	**8**

tens	ones
1	9
+3	0
4	**9**

Page 146

Anchors Away

Add. Use the code to find the answer to this riddle:
What did the pirate have to do before every trip out to sea?

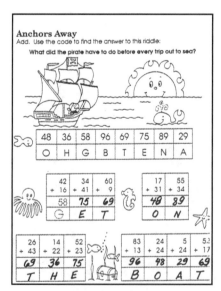

48	36	58	96	69	75	89	29
O	H	G	B	T	E	N	A

$$\begin{array}{r} 42 \\ +16 \\ \hline 58 \end{array} \quad \begin{array}{r} 34 \\ +41 \\ \hline 75 \end{array} \quad \begin{array}{r} 60 \\ +9 \\ \hline 69 \end{array}$$
G E T

$$\begin{array}{r} 17 \\ +31 \\ \hline 48 \end{array} \quad \begin{array}{r} 55 \\ +34 \\ \hline 89 \end{array}$$
O N

$$\begin{array}{r} 26 \\ +43 \\ \hline 69 \end{array} \quad \begin{array}{r} 14 \\ +22 \\ \hline 36 \end{array} \quad \begin{array}{r} 52 \\ +23 \\ \hline 75 \end{array}$$
T H E

$$\begin{array}{r} 83 \\ +13 \\ \hline 96 \end{array} \quad \begin{array}{r} 24 \\ +24 \\ \hline 48 \end{array} \quad \begin{array}{r} 5 \\ +24 \\ \hline 29 \end{array} \quad \begin{array}{r} 53 \\ +17 \\ \hline 69 \end{array}$$
B O A T

Page 147

Digital Addition

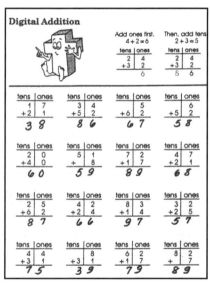

Add ones first.
$4 + 2 = 6$

tens	ones
2	4
+3	2
	6

Then, add tens
$2 + 3 = 5$

tens	ones
2	4
+3	2
5	6

tens	ones
1	7
+2	1
3	**8**

tens	ones
3	4
+5	2
8	**6**

tens	ones
	5
+6	2
6	**7**

tens	ones
	6
+5	2
5	**8**

tens	ones
2	0
+4	0
6	**0**

tens	ones
5	1
+8	
5	**9**

tens	ones
7	2
+1	7
8	**9**

tens	ones
4	7
+2	1
6	**8**

tens	ones
2	5
+6	2
8	**7**

tens	ones
4	2
+2	4
6	**6**

tens	ones
8	3
+1	4
9	**7**

tens	ones
3	2
+2	5
5	**7**

tens	ones
4	4
+3	1
7	**5**

tens	ones
	8
+3	1
3	**9**

tens	ones
6	2
+1	7
7	**9**

tens	ones
8	2
+1	7
8	**9**

Page 148

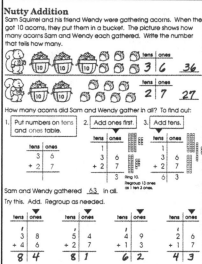

Page 149

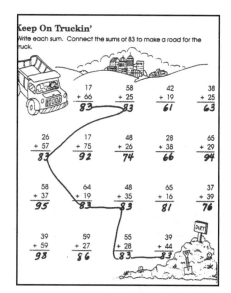

Page 150

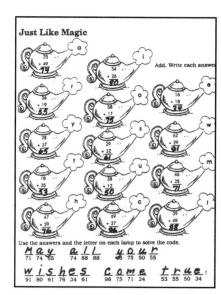

Page 151

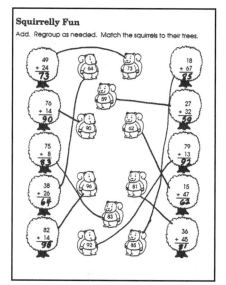

Page 152

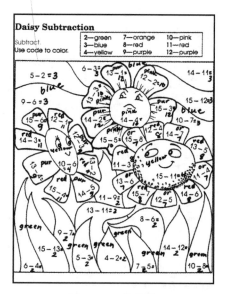

Page 153

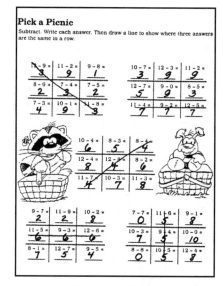

Page 154

Answer Key

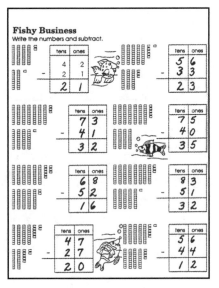

Page 155

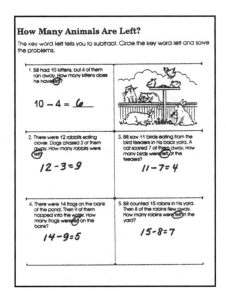

Page 156

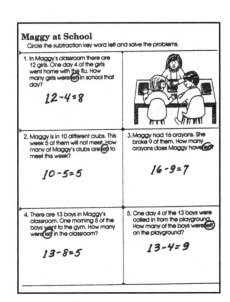

Page 157

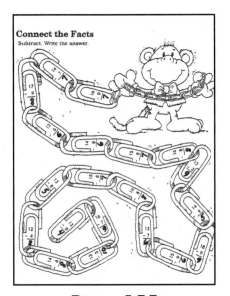

Page 158

Page 159

Page 160

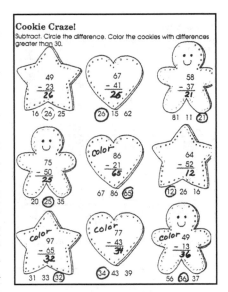

Page 161

Page 162

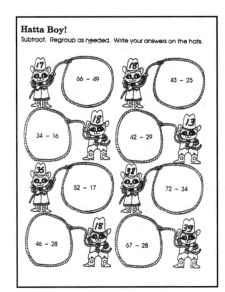

Page 163

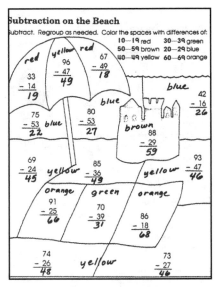

Page 164

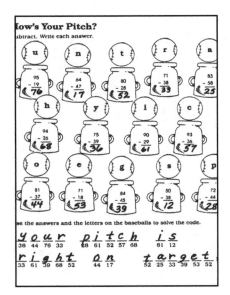

Page 165

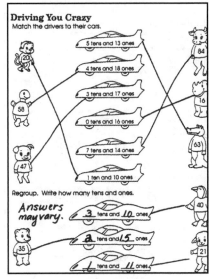

Page 166

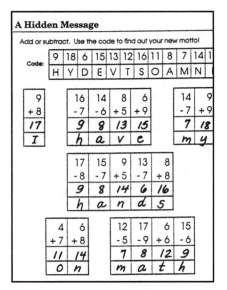

A Hidden Message

Add or subtract. Use the code to find out your new motto!

Code:

9	18	6	15	13	12	16	11	8	7	14	1
H	Y	D	E	V	T	S	O	A	M	N	I

| 9
+8
17
I | | 16
-7
9
h | 14
-6
8
a | 8
+5
13
v | 6
+9
15
e | | 14
-7
7
m | 9
+9
18
y |

| 17
-8
9
h | 15
-7
8
a | 9
+5
14
n | 13
-7
6
d | 8
+8
16
s |

| 4
+7
11
O | 6
+8
14
n | | 12
-5
7
m | 17
-9
8
a | 6
+6
12
t | 15
-6
9
h |

Page 167

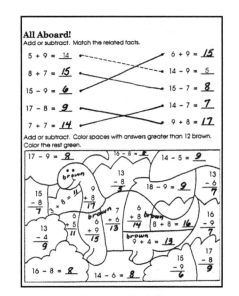

All Aboard!

Add or subtract. Match the related facts.

5 + 9 = __14__   6 + 9 = __15__
8 + 7 = __15__   14 − 9 = __5__
15 − 9 = __6__   15 − 7 = __8__
17 − 8 = __9__   14 − 7 = __7__
7 + 7 = __14__   9 + 8 = __17__

Add or subtract. Color spaces with answers greater than 12 brown. Color the rest green.

17 − 9 = __8__   16 − 8 = __8__   14 − 5 = __9__

9 + 2 = 11 brown
8 − 3 = 5
7 + 7 = 14
18 − 9 = 9
13 − 6 = 7
15 − 8 = 7
9 + 8 = 17
6 + 8 = 14 brown
8 + 8 = 16
16 − 9 = 7
13 − 4 = 9
4 + 9 = 13
brown 9 + 4 = 13
15 − 8 = 7
17 − 8 = 9

16 − 8 = __8__   14 − 6 = __8__

Page 168

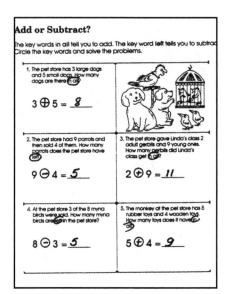

Add or Subtract?

The key words in all tell you to add. The key word left tells you to subtract. Circle the key words and solve the problems.

1. The pet store has 3 large dogs and 5 small dogs. How many dogs are there in all?

3 ⊕ 5 = __8__

2. The pet store had 9 parrots and then sold 4 of them. How many parrots does the pet store have left?

9 ⊖ 4 = __5__

3. The pet store gave Linda's class 2 adult gerbils and 9 young ones. How many gerbils did Linda's class get in all?

2 ⊕ 9 = __11__

4. At the pet store 3 of the 8 myna birds were sold. How many myna birds are left in the pet store?

8 ⊖ 3 = __5__

5. The monkey at the pet store has 5 rubber toys and 4 wooden toys. How many toys does it have in all?

5 ⊕ 4 = __9__

Page 169

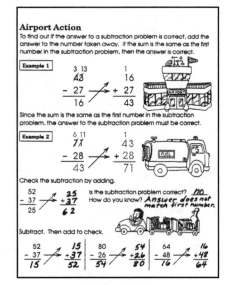

Airport Action

To find out if the answer to a subtraction problem is correct, add the answer to the number taken away. If the sum is the same as the first number in the subtraction problem, then the answer is correct.

Example 1
  3 13
  4̶3̶
− 27   1
───── + 27
  16   43

Since the sum is the same as the first number in the subtraction problem, the answer to the subtraction problem must be correct.

Example 2
  6 11
  7̶1̶
− 28   1
───── + 28
  43   71

Check the subtraction by adding.

  52   25
− 37   + 37
─────   ─────
  25   62

Is the subtraction problem correct? **no**
How do you know? **Answer does not match first number.**

Subtract. Then add to check.

  52   15 | 80   54 | 64   16
− 37   + 37 | − 26   + 26 | − 48   + 48
───── ───── | ───── ───── | ───── ─────
  15   52 | 54   80 | 16   64

Page 170

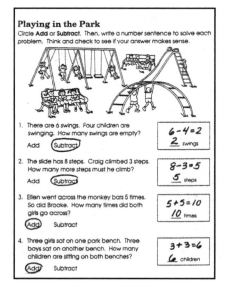

Playing in the Park

Circle **Add** or **Subtract**. Then, write a number sentence to solve each problem. Think and check to see if your answer makes sense.

1. There are 6 swings. Four children are swinging. How many swings are empty?
   Add (Subtract)
   6 − 4 = 2
   2 swings

2. The slide has 8 steps. Craig climbed 3 steps. How many more steps must he climb?
   Add (Subtract)
   8 − 3 = 5
   5 steps

3. Ellen went across the monkey bars 5 times. So did Brooke. How many times did both girls go across?
   (Add) Subtract
   5 + 5 = 10
   10 times

4. Three girls sat on one park bench. Three boys sat on another bench. How many children are sitting on both benches?
   (Add) Subtract
   3 + 3 = 6
   6 children

Page 171

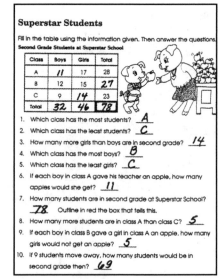

Superstar Students

Fill in the table using the information given. Then answer the questions.

Second Grade Students at Superstar School

Class	Boys	Girls	Total
A	11	17	28
B	12	15	27
C	9	14	23
Total	32	46	78

1. Which class has the most students? __A__
2. Which class has the least students? __C__
3. How many more girls than boys are in second grade? __14__
4. Which class has the most boys? __B__
5. Which class has the least girls? __C__
6. If each boy in class A gave his teacher an apple, how many apples would she get? __11__
7. How many students are in second grade at Superstar School? __78__ Outline in red the box that tells this.
8. How many more students are in class A than class C? __5__
9. If each boy in class B gave a girl in class A an apple, how many girls would not get an apple? __5__
10. If 9 students move away, how many students would be in second grade then? __69__

Page 172

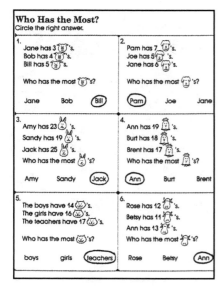

Page 173

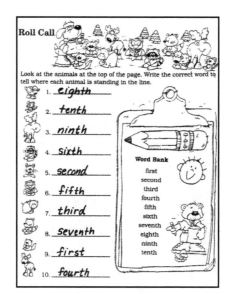

Page 174

Page 175

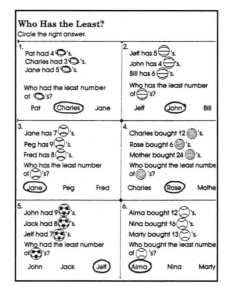

Page 176

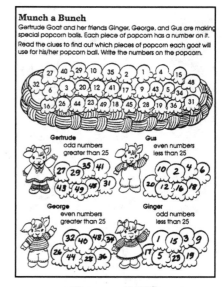

Page 177

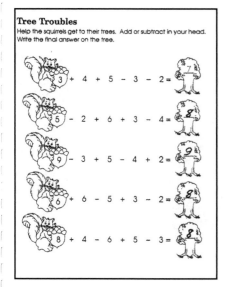

Page 178

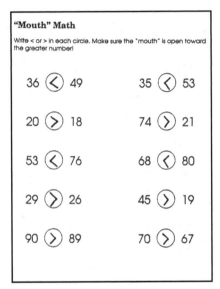

"Mouth" Math

Write < or > in each circle. Make sure the "mouth" is open toward the greater number!

36 < 49   35 < 53

20 > 18   74 > 21

53 < 76   68 < 80

29 > 26   45 > 19

90 > 89   70 > 67

Page 179

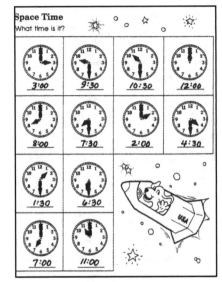

Space Time
What time is it?

3:00   9:30   10:30   12:00

8:00   7:30   2:00   4:30

1:30   6:30

7:00   11:00

Page 180

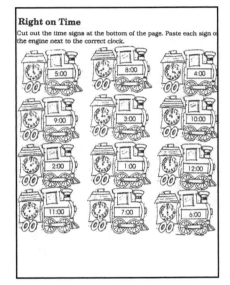

Right on Time
Cut out the time signs at the bottom of the page. Paste each sign on the engine next to the correct clock.

5:00   8:00   4:00

9:00   3:00   10:00

2:00   1:00   12:00

11:00   7:00   6:00

Page 181

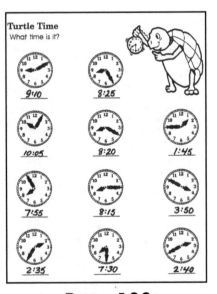

Turtle Time
What time is it?

9:10   8:25

10:05   8:20   1:45

7:55   8:15   3:50

2:35   7:30   2:40

Page 183

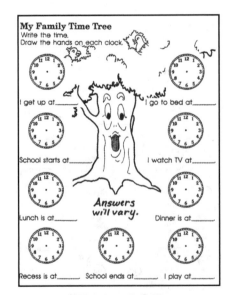

My Family Time Tree
Write the time.
Draw the hands on each clock.

I get up at____   I go to bed at____

School starts at____   I watch TV at____

Answers will vary.

Lunch is at____   Dinner is at____

Recess is at____   School ends at____   I play at____

Page 184

Time to Clean Up
Match the digital time with each clock face by cutting and pasting each lid on the correct trash can.

9:05   12:25   5:40   11:20

4:15   7:35   8:00   2:55

1:30   10:50   3:10   6:45

Page 185

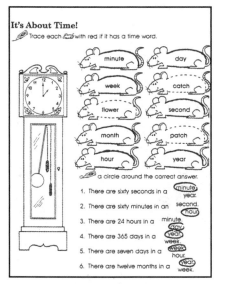

Page 187

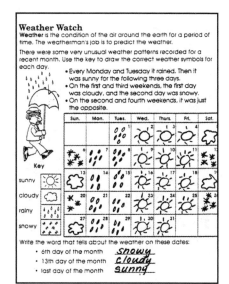

Page 188

Write the word that tells about the weather on these dates:
- 6th day of the month — snowy
- 13th day of the month — cloudy
- last day of the month — sunny

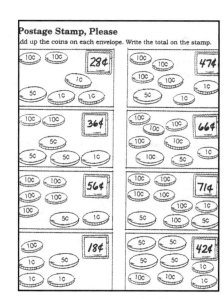

Page 189

Page 190

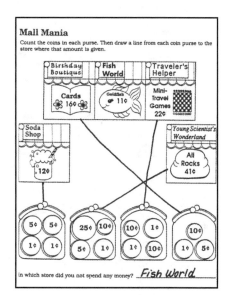

In which store did you not spend any money? *Fish World*

Page 191

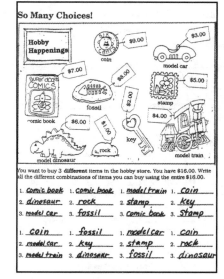

Page 192

Answer Key

Earnings Add Up!

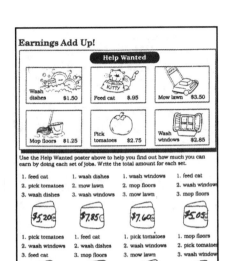

Page 193

Here's Your Order

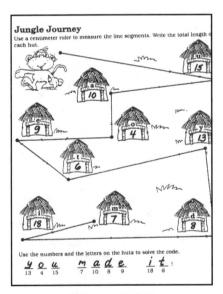

Page 194

Flowers That "Measure" Up

Cut out the centimeter ruler at the bottom of the page. Use the ruler to measure how tall each flower is from the bottom of the stem to the top of the flower. Write the answer below the bee.

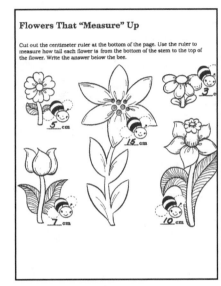

Page 195

Brush Up on Measuring!

Use your centimeter ruler to measure these brushes to the nearest centimeter.

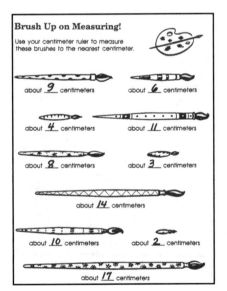

about __9__ centimeters   about __6__ centimeters

about __4__ centimeters   about __11__ centimeters

about __8__ centimeters   about __3__ centimeters

about __14__ centimeters

about __10__ centimeters   about __2__ centimeters

about __17__ centimeters

Page 197

Jungle Journey

Use a centimeter ruler to measure the line segments. Write the total length of each hut.

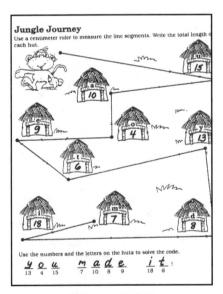

Use the numbers and the letters on the huts to solve the code.

__y__ __o__ __u__ __m__ __a__ __d__ __e__ __i__ __t__ !
13 4   15   7 10 8 9   18 6

Page 198

Gauging the Weather

Cut out the centimeter ruler at the bottom of the page. Use the ruler to measure the amount of rainfall from the bottom of the gauge to the top of the water. Write the measurement on the raindrop.

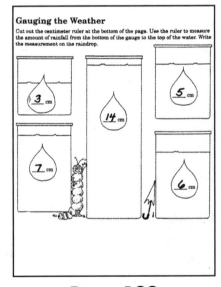

Page 199

Jumping Jellybeans

Use an inch ruler to measure the line segments. Write the total length on each candy jar.

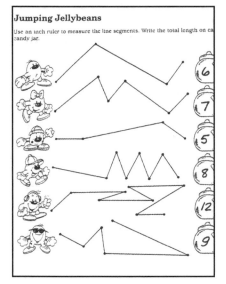

6
7
5
8
12
9

Page 201

The Inch Worm

Measure these worms to the nearest inch.

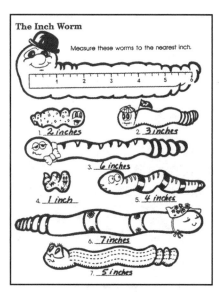

1. 2 inches
2. 3 inches
3. 6 inches
4. 1 inch
5. 4 inches
6. 7 inches
7. 5 inches

Page 202

How Big Are You?

You are getting so big! Every day, you grow a little more. Estimate how long some of your body parts are. Then, using a ruler, work with a friend to find the actual measurements.

Height
Est.
Meas.

Arm Span
Est.
Meas.

Arm Length
Est.
Meas.

Measurements will vary.

Leg Length
Est.
Meas.

Foot Length
Est.
Meas.

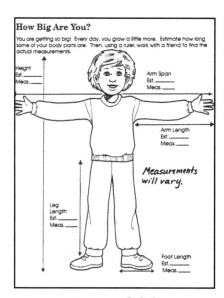

Page 203

How Far Is It?

Use your ruler to measure each distance on the map. Then use the letters on the tires and your answers to solve the message at the bottom of the page.

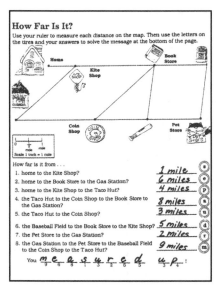

Home
Kite Shop
Book Store
Coin Shop
Pet Store

Scale 1 inch = 1 mile

How far is it from . . .

1. home to the Kite Shop? — 1 mile
2. home to the Book Store to the Gas Station? — 6 miles
3. home to the Kite Shop to the Taco Hut? — 4 miles
4. the Taco Hut to the Coin Shop to the Book Store to the Gas Station? — 8 miles
5. the Taco Hut to the Coin Shop? — 3 miles
6. the Baseball Field to the Book Store to the Kite Shop? — 5 miles
7. the Pet Store to the Gas Station? — 2 miles
8. the Gas Station to the Pet Store to the Baseball Field to the Coin Shop to the Taco Hut? — 9 miles

You m e a s u r e d   u p !
9 6 5 1 3 4 2 5 3   4 P

Page 204

Liquid Limits

Draw a line from the containers on the left to the containers on the right that will hold the same amount of liquid. **Hint:** 2 pints = 1 quart.

Answers will vary.

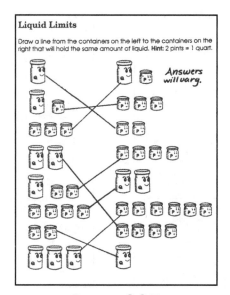

Page 205

Sew What?

A favorite activity of colonial women and girls was getting together for a quilting bee. The quilts, made from scraps of linen, wool, and cotton, were frequently sewn together in a pattern.

Look carefully at the pattern in the unfinished quilt below. Then continue the pattern by drawing pictures in the blank sections to complete the quilt.

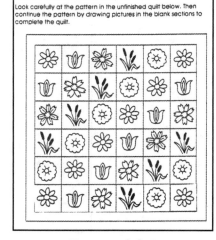

Page 206

Shape Sort

Color the ones in each row that are the same size and shape. Write T for triangle, R for rectangle and S for square

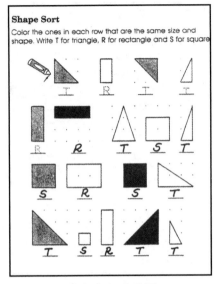

Page 207

Sea Shapes

Find the shapes and color them using the code.

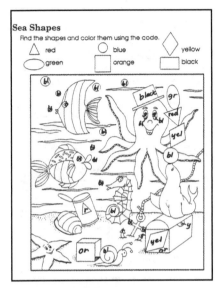

Page 208

Equal and Unequal Parts

Cut out each shape below along the solid lines. Then fold the shape on the dotted lines. Do you get equal or unequal parts? Sort the shapes into two piles: those with equal parts and those with unequal parts.

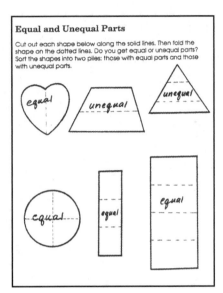

Page 209

Shaded Shapes

Draw line from fraction to correct shape.

$\frac{1}{3}$ shaded

$\frac{2}{4}$ shaded

$\frac{1}{4}$ shaded

$\frac{1}{2}$ shaded

$\frac{3}{4}$ shaded

$\frac{2}{3}$ shaded

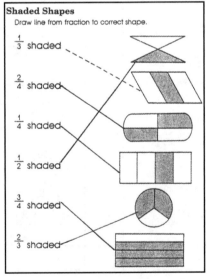

Page 211

Fraction Food

Count the equal parts. Circle the fraction that names one of the parts.

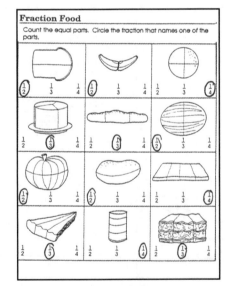

Page 212

Answer Key

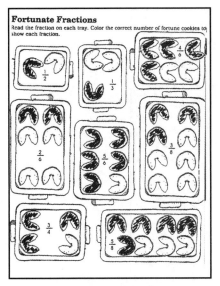

Page 213

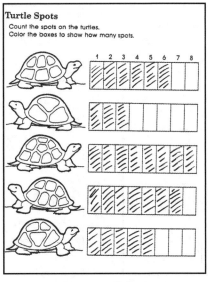

Page 214

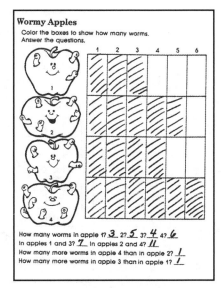

Page 215

Page 216

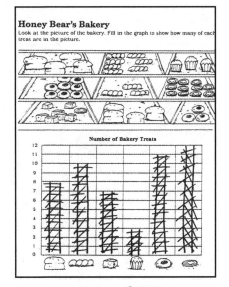

Page 217

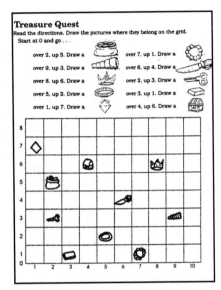

Page 218

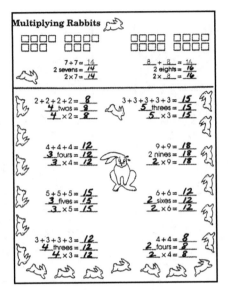

Page 219

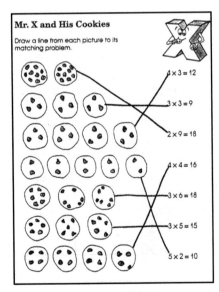

Page 220

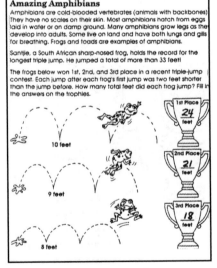

Page 221